HOW TO OPEN AND OPERATE
A HOME-BASED
DESKTOP PUBLISHING BUSINESS

HOW TO OPEN AND OPERATE A HOME-BASED

Desktop Publishing

BUSINESS

by Louise Kursmark

The Globe Pequot Press

OLD SAYBROOK, CONNECTICUT

TO BOB

who started it all with a simple suggestion thirteen years ago

Cover and text design by Nancy Freeborn

Library of Congress Cataloging-in-Publication Data is available.

Manufactured in the United States of America
First Edition/First Printing

CONTENTS

ACKNOWLEDGMENTS / viii

INTRODUCTION / ix

1 BEGINNING THE JOURNEY / 1

Desktop Publishing Defined / 2
A Bit of History / 2
Who Does DTP? / 3
What is DTP Used For? / 4
Home-Based: Why it Makes Sense / 5
Home-Based: Potential Pitfalls / 5
The Journey Begins / 6

2 ASSESSING YOURSELF AND YOUR ABILITIES / 7

Technical/Professional Skills / 7
Business-Management Skills / 10
Working From Home / 13
Personal Characteristics / 15
Assessing Your Skills / 17

3 PLANNING FOR SUCCESS / 35

Gathering Information / 35
Naming Your Business / 36
Legal and Regulatory Issues / 38
Structuring Your Business / 39
Analyzing Your Competitors / 41

Selecting Your Service Mix/Identifying Niches / 42
Determining Your Start-Up Needs / 45
Determining Your Rate Structure / 62
Writing a Business Plan / 72
Starting Your Business Part-Time or with Limited Resources / 76

4 SETTING UP YOUR OFFICE / 81

Selecting Your Office Space / 81
Client Drop Boxes / 84
Safety Issues / 85
Office Essentials / 86
Health, Comfort, and Ergonomic Issues / 88

5 MARKETING AND SELLING YOUR SERVICES / 91

Attracting Clients / 93
Retaining Clients / 111
Increasing Sales to Existing Clients / 115
Developing Marketing Materials / 121
Developing and Using A Portfolio / 124

6 GETTING THE WORK DONE / 127

Organizing and Setting Priorities / 128
Gathering and Maintaining Client Information / 133
Structuring Work Time / 140
Keeping Order / 141
Managing Client Files / 148
Financial Record Keeping / 149
Managing Your Cash Flow / 151
Dealing with Computer Problems / 154
Scheduling Appointments / 156
Converting Inquiries to Sales / 158
Effective Client Presentations / 162
Preparing Proposals and Estimates / 165

7 WORKING WITH DESKTOP PUBLISHING / 169

Creating Distinctive Documents / 170
Typography and Style Guidelines / 171
Design Guidelines / 175
Accepting and Providing Disks / 176
Determining the Price of a Job / 180
Developing a Process / 197

8 MANAGING YOUR BUSINESS AT HOME / 201

Making Time for Yourself / 202
Housekeeping / 202
Separating Business and Home Lives / 203
Balancing Your Work and Home Lives / 205

9 LIVING YOUR VISION / 211

Managing the Growth of Your Business / 211
The Future of Desktop Publishing / 213

APPENDIX / 217

Books / 217
Credit Card / 218
Guides and Catalogs / 218
Organizations / 219
Periodicals / 219
Specialty Papers / 220

INDEX / 223

ACKNOWLEDGMENTS

I owe thanks and appreciation to many, many people who have contributed to my accomplishments in both my desktop publishing business and the writing of this book:

. . . Kathy Keshemberg and Carla Culp—thanks, "gals," for advice, inspiration, encouragement, gossip, lots of laughs, and good times from coast to coast

. . . my clients, most especially Alan and Debbie Slobodnik; Irving Stackpole; John Connors; Scott Kent; and Bob, Cindy, David, and Keith Killian, all of whom helped me learn, gave me opportunities to grow, and were a constant delight to work with

. . . Keith Killian and Rose DiSanto, who took the time to share helpful information on DTP-vendor relationships

. . . professional colleagues in Boston, Cincinnati, and throughout the United States who shared their time, their opinions, and the thrills and chills of the DTP business

. . . Mace Lewis, my editor, for guidance and encouragement (and pizza, beer, and baseball talk)

. . . Jan Melnik, my best friend for twenty-five years (!), professional colleague, fellow writer, and the inspiration for my original book proposal . . . looking forward to what we'll do in the next twenty-five

. . . my parents, Gordon and Rita McGuire, who gave each of their eight children the belief that we could do *anything* if we really wanted to

. . . my children, Meredith and Matt, without whom my life would be incomplete—I love you, and thanks for putting up with me in my more crazed states

. . . my husband, Bob, who always encourages me to reach for the stars—and then builds me a rocket ship—thanks for your belief, practical assistance, and love

. . . and in loving memory of my grandmother, Cecilia Krawczyk, "Gram" to the world . . . who modeled good manners and selflessness for ninety years

INTRODUCTION

If they asked me, I could write a book . . .

—LORENZ HART

ell, they asked. Out of the blue, months after I had submitted a proposal, I received a phone call from Mace Lewis, Associate Editor at The Globe Pequot Press, informing me that my proposal to write this book had been approved. I eagerly accepted the challenge and agreed to a deadline—then hung up wondering if I had lost my wits. At that time I was just beginning to plan for a major life transition—the relocation of my family and business from Boston to Cincinnati. My husband, Bob, had accepted a job transfer, and I had three and a half months to sell my business in Massachusetts and prepare to establish it all over again in Cincinnati, while also managing my children's school transition, selling one house and overseeing the building of another, decorating, purchasing furniture, making detailed moving plans, and squeezing in "must-do" New England activities before we moved. On top of all this, I had just committed to write a book!

Since I am by nature an optimist and also respond *really* well to deadlines, I figured I would somehow get everything done . . . and I did. In fact, the writing of this book was an excellent foundation for my new beginning, reminding me of all that would be involved in a new-business start-up.

My business, initially named Secretarial Services Unlimited, started in 1982 as a typing service in those pre–personal computer days. I set up my rented IBM Selectric in my infant daughter's bedroom and placed a small classified ad in the local paper. My first month in business resulted in one job and a gross income of $25—but I had begun! As an English major with a strong secretarial background and a good eye for detail, I enjoyed using my skills to provide a high level of service to my small but growing client base. By 1983 I had moved up to a memory typewriter (huge, heavy, slow, and limited by today's standards, but a marvel compared to the typewriter), and in 1986 I plunged into the heady new world of desktop publishing on the Macintosh. My husband was the catalyst for this, as he had become familiar with the capabilities of this new computer and was convinced I could put it to good use in my secretarial business. That year also marked my first writing venture, as a friend and I cowrote a self-published guide to Disney World (*Disney World with Kids: Making the Most of Your Family Vacation*), and the Macintosh computer and laser printer, along with PageMaker software, were our tools for producing work of a professional quality that was simply not available to small businesses prior to their advent.

The summer of '87, when our book was published, was also memorable because of the birth of my son, Matt. It was interesting running a business during my pregnancy. I was fortunate to have a healthy and joyous nine months, and my clients seemed to enjoy sharing in my anticipation . . . and commenting on my growth! I continued to work up to and past his due date, starting every job thinking, "I better do this right away just in case . . ." On the morning of August 20, discovering that I was beginning labor, I whipped down to the office to complete a few last-minute tasks, then chatted with a client who came to pick up some completed work just as we were leaving for the hospital. Matt and I came home two days later, and I clearly remember feeling slightly bored, wandering into my office to complete a quick mailing-label project, and wondering what on earth people *did* if they didn't work at home! Predictably, my boredom was soon interrupted by two solid months of colic, but somehow we survived . . . and thrived.

Now I find it difficult to imagine any better way of working than running my own business in my home. I love the control and flexibility, the tremendous variety of projects, the truly wonderful clients . . . and the money. My income is significantly higher than it would have been had I stayed in the corporate business world. I can control what I make by adjusting the hours that I work—I might put in a lot of extra effort and achieve a big payoff, or choose to cut back during the summer while my children are at home. The choice is mine! I make the decisions and reap the rewards—or, occasionally, suffer the consequences! I decide what to charge; whether I want to take on a project; how to handle a complaint; what equipment to buy. There's no red tape, no approval process, no inflexible policies. There are down sides, as in any endeavor. During start-up, there's the worry that there won't be enough work to keep busy; and when things do take off, there's the stress of being busy all the time. There's no one but me to accept responsibility when things go wrong or to do the dirty work, the less enjoyable tasks. But I've kept on running my business because I find satisfaction and fulfillment in every working day.

I would be remiss if I didn't mention my husband's contribution to the business. I am extremely fortunate to be married to someone who is convinced I can do just about anything and who consistently supports and encourages me. I'm also in the truly privileged position of having in Bob my own personal computer consultant. (Many of my friends in the business are jealous and tell me they want a Bob, too!) From the beginning he has assumed the time-consuming tasks of researching and purchasing equipment, installing software, backing up files, resolving conflicts, and troubleshooting. Without his invaluable, eminently practical assistance, I would have had to spend countless hours on these tasks. Bob is also a good sounding board for new ideas and a thoughtful listener when I'm wrestling with a problem.

My children, too, have had a profound effect on my business. They're the reason for it all—I wanted to avoid the full-time day-care routine while at the same time continuing my career, which I truly enjoyed. They've never known me to do anything *except* work at home. They're amazingly equable about the whole thing; it's just something Mom does. I believe they appreciate the advantages—the fact that I'm much more available to spend time with them than if I held a full-time job outside the home—in spite of having to share my time and attention with my third, very demanding, "baby"—my business, Best Impression.

As I write this Introduction, I'm preparing to start the whole thing all over again. I wish I could tell you that having written the book, having done it all before, I'll make all the right moves, avoid the mistakes, and immediately achieve a high level of success. But, in fact, I'm in the same boat as you who are reading this book: I'm starting a new business, facing new challenges. And we will make mistakes, you and I; but they'll be our *own* mistakes, and we'll learn from them and continue on our journey toward home-based desktop publishing success. I know—and you'll learn—that it's an incredibly satisfying journey. I consider it a privilege to be your companion along the way.

CHAPTER ONE

BEGINNING THE JOURNEY

A journey of a thousand miles must begin with a single step.   —**LAO-TZU**

Ten short years ago, *desktop publishing* was a term familiar to few and practiced by even fewer. Today this technology has completely revolutionized the way we produce printed pages. Still in its infancy, desktop publishing has created the livelihood of some 300,000 professional desktop designers in the United States and directly affected probably three times that many in some aspect of their job. And the technology continues to expand—daily, it seems. Opportunities for employment—and self-employment—are growing.

This book has been written to guide the home-based desktop publishing entrepreneur through the many stages of assessing, planning, setting up, growing the business, and making it work. The advice and information are drawn from my thirteen-plus years of running a home-based business—including ten years as a desktop publishing professional. You'll learn what has worked, for me and for others. I'll share sales, marketing, and client relationship tips, along with practical, hands-on advice about day-to-day operations in a home-based enterprise of this kind. Equally important, you can benefit from my mistakes and learn what *not* to do!

You have taken the first, most difficult step—making the decision to own your own business. To be a professional desktop publisher requires a set of specific skills. Add to that the requirements to be a business owner and manager and to handle the demands of running a business from your home, and it's clear that this will be a challenge and an adventure! This book is designed to serve as a guide on your journey and to assist you toward your goal of running a successful home-based desktop publishing business. May you enjoy every step along the way!

DESKTOP PUBLISHING DEFINED

Desktop publishing (DTP) is the term for a system of hardware and software that allows the user to assemble, manipulate, and control all phases of a publication—type, illustrations, photographs, charts and graphs, colors, etc.—electronically rather than mechanically.

A BIT OF HISTORY

The term *desktop publishing* was coined by Paul Brainerd, the founder of Aldus Corporation—the company that developed PageMaker, the first page-layout software for the personal computer. PageMaker was introduced in 1985, a year after the Apple Macintosh computer had appeared on the scene with its point-and-click graphical user interface, its "WYSIWYG" ("what you see is what you get") use of type and graphics, and its friendly approach to personal computing. Equally essential to the emergence of desktop publishing was the development of the PostScript printing language by Adobe Corporation and the desktop laser printer, also by Apple Computer. The combined availability of these products in 1985 signaled the beginning of a revolution in the publishing world and the creation of a new industry.

By today's standards, the capabilities of the early computers and software were laughable. The first Macs had 128 kilobytes of RAM—about an eighth of a megabyte!—while desktop publishing systems today typically contain anywhere from 16 to 128 megabytes. Typesetters and graphic designers initially disparaged the capabilities of the new systems and doubted their ability to produce professional-quality type and graphics. Today, of course, all that has changed. Traditional typesetters are a dying breed, and graphic designers increasingly are utilizing sophisticated computer applications.

Recognizing the potential for desktop publishing, both hardware and software companies have worked continuously—and competitively—since 1985 to improve quality, add features and capabilities, and bring their systems to the professional level available today.

WHO DOES DTP?

Desktop publishing technology is used in companies large and small, by freelance and self-employed individuals, and by businesses as their main line of work or as a single profit center. It can be useful to any and every individual and type of business!

Although desktop publishing is becoming increasingly user-friendly, and more and more people are becoming familiar with DTP terminology and capabilities, there are professionals in this field as in any other. These professionals are the most knowledgeable and expert in at least some phase of desktop publishing and utilize the technology as a principal component of their work.

Desktop publishing professionals work in a variety of environments, including this representative sampling:

- graphics design firm

- DTP/publishing center of a large corporation

- service bureau providing DTP design services, assistance to other desktop publishers, and high-resolution output from a variety of devices

- newspaper, magazine, or other publishing enterprise

- design/publication department of small graphics-intensive firm (e.g., real estate office, architectural firm, marketing and promotions company, advertising agency)

- print shop that provides its own typesetting and does desktop publishing for customers as an additional profit center

- large self-service computer/copy center with staff available to assist customers as well as provide direct DTP services
- word processing/secretarial service that also provides DTP services
- home- or office-based desktop publisher and designer

Most desktop publishers starting their own businesses come from a background of either word processing or graphic design and generally have well-developed desktop publishing skills. Others start with merely a facility for computers, a good eye for design, and a determination to own their own business. (See chapter 2 for a discussion of required skills, how and where to get them, and how to succeed using your own specific strengths.)

WHAT IS DTP USED FOR?

Desktop publishing is used to produce a vast array of incredibly varied documents. Following are a few of the products that can be created utilizing desktop publishing:

- business forms
- marketing mailers
- stationery, business cards
- advertisements
- brochures
- newsletters
- catalogs
- proposals
- manuscripts

- presentation materials
- menus
- price lists
- flyers
- CD and cassette liners
- calendars
- posters
- report covers
- logos

As is evident from this list, virtually every business and individual can use desktop publishing for some purpose. Some DTP business owners choose to specialize, seeking and accepting only those projects that fit their niche. Others are generalists, handling any and every assignment that comes their way and enjoying the diversity.

HOME-BASED: WHY IT MAKES SENSE

Operating a home-based business is very attractive for a variety of personal reasons. Juggling busy family schedules, raising young children, being available to family members on a regular basis can all be simpler if you are working at home. Work time can be fit around family commitments, and although many who do so find themselves working at midnight or 5:00 A.M., most consider it a satisfactory trade-off! Some businesses seem naturally suited to being operated from a home-based office. Desktop publishing is one of these, for a number of reasons:

- Despite high equipment costs, the profession can be very rewarding financially, even for a one-person business—unlike some businesses, which require large volumes and, consequently, increases in staff.

- Clients can be handled professionally by phone, fax, courier, and the occasional visit to a client's office. Extensive client meeting space and an impressive office environment are not typically required.

- Working alone, away from distracting office environments, can be very conducive to creative work.

- A typical client mix includes businesses, both large and small, as well as individuals with a variety of needs. Serving this varied client base can help ensure steady work with projects of all sizes to fill available time.

- Opportunities for education and networking are readily available through computer groups, professional associations, and other organizations, reducing any sense of isolation.

- The growing acceptance of home businesses helps to cast a favorable and professional light on a home-based DTP service.

HOME-BASED: POTENTIAL PITFALLS

Of course, in addition to advantages there may be disadvantages—real or perceived—in operating a desktop publishing business from home:

- Some home-based business owners find it difficult, if not impossible, to get away from their work. Consequently, family life can suffer.

- Family members may feel resentful when interrupted by ringing telephones, incoming faxes, and the business owner's distraction when working on an important project. Having the support of your family members will be crucial to your success in operating your business at home.

- You may be plagued by unprofessional office interruptions—babies crying, dogs barking, televisions blaring, children picking up the extension while you're on a critical client call. (See chapter 8 for strategies to minimize these disruptions!)

- Some individuals, including potential clients, may feel your business is less professional or less serious if it is operated from home. This stereotype is dimming, however, as being home-based becomes more common and these individuals have increased opportunity to work with professional, home-based-business owners.

Taking pleasure in the advantages your home business has to offer and making the most of your flexibility and independence can go a long way toward minimizing any possible disadvantages.

THE JOURNEY BEGINS

Your first step on the journey to desktop publishing success has already been taken—you have made the decision. Congratulations! This book will provide you with stepping-stones to guide you along the sometimes difficult—but always rewarding—path.

Let's begin!

CHAPTER TWO

ASSESSING YOURSELF AND YOUR ABILITIES

> Knowledge is of two kinds. We know a subject ourselves, or we know where we can find information upon it.
>
> — **SAMUEL JOHNSON**

utcher, baker, candlestick maker . . . running your own business requires you to fill a wide variety of roles. The basic skills you'll need, of course, relate to performing the work of desktop publishing. But since you are the business owner and manager as well as the production worker, your job description will be very comprehensive! Let's explore the requirements and talk about some options for locating or acquiring skills you don't already have.

TECHNICAL/PROFESSIONAL SKILLS

Your desktop publishing expertise may very well be the basis for starting your own business. If that's the case, you are well aware of the diverse skills needed to be an expert in this field:

- *Mastery of page layout and graphics programs* (most commonly Adobe PageMaker, QuarkXPress, or Ventura Publisher, plus Adobe

Illustrator, Macromedia FreeHand, Adobe Photoshop, or other drawing/image editing programs). You will need to know your chosen programs backwards, forwards, and inside out. You will also need to know how other documents and programs work with yours and how to achieve a variety of outputs from your file. The entire electronic publishing industry is something you should be familiar with. Whether you provide services at all levels or not, you do need to know what's available and where to get it. You will need to speak the same language as your knowledgeable clients and be the expert for those clients whose knowledge of desktop publishing is limited.

Example . . . *A large corporate client asks you if their employee manual, which is typically updated every two or three years, would be better prepared using PageMaker or WordPerfect. You analyze the project and conclude that PageMaker's graphics capabilities and long-document-handling strengths make its use preferable. After completing the project, you offer to output the text in WordPerfect format so the client can update it over the years and resubmit the revised text file when they're ready to reprint the manual.*

- *Computer expertise in related areas.* Your skills in scanning graphics, defining details such as trapping, bleeds, and color separations, and assembling needed elements from a variety of computer-generated sources will enable you to complete complex projects and get the most from your considerable investment in hardware and software.

   Example . . . *Your client comes to you with a process-color-printed graphic for use in a catalog you are preparing for him to have reproduced using only spot color. You scan the graphic, recolor it with the appropriate spot color, and place it in your page-layout program.*

- *Graphic design abilities.* Since desktop publishing most often involves a combination of type and graphics, the desktop publisher needs to be a desktop designer as well. Your ability to lay out a page in a manner that is fresh and attractive and conveys the client's desired message is a skill that will be valued and needed by your clients. Creating original art, whether on the computer or manually, is a unique service you can offer to your clients and use to improve the quality and originality of your work.

Example . . . *Your client likes to rough out her brochures on her own computer, to give her an idea of the length of her copy. She presents you with her laser-printed draft and the file on disk. Using her words and your design skills, you prepare a brochure basically conforming to her effort but with your professional design and layout. Taking into consideration her audience and her budget, you create a series of original cartoons for use on each panel of the brochure.*

■ *Knowledge of printing operations.* Knowing how your original is going to be reproduced is of vital importance from the very beginning. You need to have an understanding of the printing process to be used and the ability to adapt your work so that it conforms with the printer's requirements. Considering this critical data at the time you start the project will result in fewer problems at the final printing and assembling stages. Your design will need to be in conformance with the client's budget and the print shop's limitations.

Example . . . *A client with a tight budget presents you with his idea for a brochure design. It includes three colors and graphics that are printed right to the edge of the page (bleeds). After reviewing the design details and budget, you recommend that your client use a two-panel brochure so that the bleeds will not require a larger-than-standard size paper and also suggest that the three-color effect might be achieved by using only two colors plus tints (screens).*

■ *Typography and typesetting skills.* You will need a full understanding of fonts, leading, kerning, and tracking. You'll need to be a wizard at tabs and a master of preparing text so that it is clear, comprehensible, and attractive. Mastering the text-handling features of your page-layout program will be an essential task.

Example . . . *A client presents you with a twelve-page, computer-generated draft of a price list and requests you to reformat it so that it can be printed front and back on one 8½-x 11-inch sheet. Your skill in selecting fonts, adjusting spacing, and using creative techniques to make specific text stand out results in a great-looking price list that is easy to read and simple to use. Your client is thrilled.*

- *Editorial skills.* Valuable assets to a desktop publishing business include a keen eye for correct language—improper word usage, non-parallel construction, and spelling errors—along with knowledge of grammar, sentence construction, and proper use of commas, apostrophes, quotation marks, and other punctuation.

  Example . . . *Your competitor down the street has a strict policy of "what we see is what you get"—work is prepared exactly as written by the client. Your clients, on the other hand, know that you will apply your expertise to ensure their work is correct, whether or not that's the way they wrote it. You amass a sizable stable of clients willing to pay extra for you to proofread, edit, and correct their writing while desktop-publishing their documents.*

- *Typing/word processing.* Material for use in desktop-published documents may arrive in your office in a variety of ways: on disk, typed or word processed, on cassette tape, legibly handwritten, or even scribbled on scraps of paper in a faint pencil scrawl. Your job includes getting that text into the computer. Having outstanding word processing skills will enable you to get this job done quickly and efficiently. Additionally, knowing how you are eventually going to use the material means that you can enter it appropriately so that minimal or no reformatting is required.

  Example . . . *A client presents you with the challenge of transforming six hours of interviews into one three-panel marketing brochure whose content will include quotes and other information from the tapes. Since your typing speed is ninety-plus words per minute, you are able to transcribe the tapes within a few days and go right to the task of editing the interviews and pulling out appropriate quotes. Your client is impressed when you present a first draft of the brochure within a week of being given the assignment.*

BUSINESS-MANAGEMENT SKILLS

Now it's time to put on your business owner's hat to review the skills required to actually operate the business:

- *Scheduling and coordinating.* In a typical week you might be called upon to keep on top of project deadlines, schedule client meetings, remember to prepare and send out your quarterly marketing mailer, and follow up on items being printed. With a project that requires contributions from the client, an independent graphic designer, and a service bureau providing high-resolution scanning, you're the puppet master keeping the strings straight and the puppets dancing. Don't forget to allot time to keep up with general business and industry-specific periodicals. And of course you have to figure out how to cram twelve hours of work (due tomorrow!) into a ten-hour day. Each business owner has his or her own methods for keeping order and keeping track. Since you will be working for numerous clients, it will be more difficult to keep order than in a typical corporate environment.

Develop systems well suited to your own strengths and weaknesses in this area. Organizational aids include to-do lists (daily, weekly, long-range), computerized calendar and reminder programs, day-planner systems, forms for garnering client data, and a variety of filing systems. (See chapter 6 for sample forms to help you gather and organize necessary information.) In crucial moments you will thank yourself for being well organized and able to lay your hands on pertinent information.

■ *Record-keeping* requirements may include preparing tax and payroll forms, billing and invoicing, keeping track of accounts receivable, writing checks and recording expenses, and determining your business's profitability. In this area, again, you will reap large dividends by setting up systems that allow you to complete these tasks easily and efficiently. Here, too, your computer can help you, with financial-management and record-keeping software that is inexpensive, widely available, and easy to use.

■ *Marketing and selling* your services are naturally of prime importance! You will be responsible for all aspects of "getting the word out" about your business—preparing, placing, and paying for advertising; writing and disseminating press releases; creating marketing materials and establishing a direct-mail schedule; responding to phone inquiries; meeting with prospective clients; preparing and following up on proposals; and a myriad of other tasks associated with this critical business function.

For many business owners, marketing and sales responsibilities cause the most anxiety. It is typical for sole proprietors to feel confident in their ability to do the work but not in their skill at selling their services. The important thing to remember is that you can devise a marketing and sales strategy that suits your own abilities and personality. You do not need to make cold calls in order to have a successful business. (I'm proof of that!) Neither do you have to join networking groups or make presentations to community organizations—unless these are particular strengths of yours. Chapter 5 discusses a variety of ways to market your business—methods that have been proven by successful business owners and will work for you, too.

■ *Maintaining client relationships* will be an important area in which to invest your time and energy. You will be the one responding to complaints and problems as well as (graciously!) accepting compliments for a job well done. It will be your job to keep in touch with clients to maintain the relationship you worked hard to establish.

■ *Allocating resources/purchasing.* It's your job to research and purchase new equipment, maintain an inventory of office supplies (so you don't run out of paper while completing a major project at 6:00 A.M.), stay on top of your cash flow, and determine how you will amass necessary funds for major purchases.

■ *Managing computer operations.* Unless you are fortunate enough to have a Bob, as I do (you can read about him in the Introduction), you will be the person responsible for backing up your files, installing new software, sorting out operating-system conflicts, deciding on new software purchases and determining if you have the memory capacity to handle them, staying on top of software upgrades, and in general serving as a computer maintenance operator for your business. These vital tasks are essential to keeping your main piece of business equipment—your computer—running smoothly and providing you with the best possible performance.

■ *Keeping up with business.* There will be no one but you to keep aware of what's going on in your field, through reading appropriate periodicals, attending conferences and networking meetings, and staying alert to what's new and how it will affect your business. Keeping an eye on business trends means you will be prepared for new, profitable opportunities. (Think about the folks who installed the first faxes and profited handsomely before these machines became a presence in every office.) Since your specialty is desktop publishing, you need to remain slightly ahead of the pack in terms of capabilities and knowledge. If you provide only the services that are available in most business offices, you are decreasing the chance that a client will need to use your services.

WORKING FROM HOME

Operating your business from a home-based office brings into play some factors that are simply not present in office-based locations. The way you respond to challenges in this area can be critical to both the success of your business and the happiness of your household.

- *Managing interruptions and distractions.* Even if you do not have children at home, the usual demands of home life will occasionally intrude into your business. You will need to set up schedules to minimize distractions and perhaps work unorthodox hours to get the work done when you have uninterrupted time. Although family members will need to understand rules about interrupting you (especially when you have clients in the office), you will want to avoid making them feel less important than your business.

- *Productivity.* Many of us who work from home find we are significantly more productive than in an office environment—especially when we are solely responsible for our business's profits! Some individuals, however, find it hard to get motivated to work when they can, instead, do some yard work, play computer games, or sit enjoying the morning paper and a second cup of coffee. If you find that getting down to work is a problem for you, it may be helpful to institute a formal schedule of office hours. Knowing you are expected to be in the office from 8:00 A.M. to 4:00 P.M. may keep you away from the television, vacuum cleaner, or time-wasting errands. For many home-based-business owners, however, one of the attractions is being able to set your own hours and work whenever you wish (6:00 A.M. or 6:00 P.M., Sunday at midnight or Monday at noon). If you are one who responds well to deadlines, you will find that the work itself is a powerful motivator, and once you have gotten through the start-up stage and are busy on a regular basis, any nonproductive activity will decrease naturally due to the necessity of completing projects on time.

■ *Isolation.* Again, many home-based-business owners thrive in the solitary splendor of their home offices. The need for regular "people contact" can be satisfied by client visits, telephone calls, and regular professional or networking meetings. For some, though, the need for frequent human interaction comes as an unwelcome surprise! One entrepreneur I know found that he intensely disliked working alone at home for long periods, so he restructured his consulting business to allow for more client interaction and also rented a downtown office and divided his time between his two business locations.

■ *Establishing a professional image.* The most important factors in your professional image are your own attitude and behavior. Regardless of whether you are in a business suit or a bathing suit (caught by a client who unexpectedly drops by), a professional demeanor and businesslike attitude will make it clear that you are, in fact, a professional running a "real" business. Working at home also gives you the advantage of having your complete wardrobe right at hand, making it a simple matter to slip into a jacket or change out of shorts when a client is expected. It is wise to act normally if you are surprised by a client when you are not exactly "dressed for success." Acting embarrassed or apologetic will only call attention to your attire and away from the client's business. Some lapses in wardrobe, housekeeping, or children's behavior will inevitably occur. Your ability to remain calm, in control, and unflustered when this happens will go a long way toward establishing your professionalism.

PERSONAL CHARACTERISTICS

Certain attributes of your personality and work style can help or hinder your success in running a home-based service business. Consider your attitude toward the following:

- *Customer-service commitment.* The most successful businesses of any kind are those that provide outstanding service to their customers. One of the advantages of a small business is that the client has direct contact with the owner and feels "personally" cared for throughout the relationship. It will be to your benefit to exploit this advantage by making customer service and strong client relationships a hallmark of your company.

- *Interpersonal skills.* Do you enjoy working directly with a variety of clients? Are you able to establish a rapport and maintain a positive, friendly, yet businesslike relationship with many diverse individuals? How do you handle complaints and criticism? Are you able to focus on the customer's need and rise above your natural defensive reaction? Do you feel you will be able to handle difficult or demanding clients effectively? Can you work with subcontractors, vendors, and other businesses so that you get what you want while maintaining a pleasant and mutually beneficial business relationship? If your interpersonal skills are very strong, you will have an advantage in handling the many "people" issues that naturally arise in a one-person, home-based business, and you will thrive on the diversity. If, on the other hand, you do not view your interaction skills as a particular strength, you may be able to focus your business so that you deal with fewer clients—for example, by specializing in large outsourced corporate projects such as employee manuals, business-forms redesign, or newsletters. "Know thyself" is an excellent adage to follow in this area; it is *your* business, and you should be comfortable and confident operating it.

- *Time management.* The standard response to the time management dilemma is, of course, "I don't have any time to manage!" And it will, indeed, feel that way at times. When you are balancing a work life and a home life, particularly if you are working around children's schedules, it's critical to make the best possible use of the time you do have available. Most people who are successful at running a home-based business learn very quickly to use productively whatever pockets of time they can find and to minimize unnecessary activities.

■ *Decision making.* Every decision, from the most mundane to the most significant, will be made by you. You must develop the ability to obtain and analyze the necessary data, make your decision, act on it, then review and assess the results. You must strike a balance between acting too swiftly and being paralyzed into inaction for fear of making the wrong decision.

■ *Health, strength, and stamina.* These factors should not be overlooked. The success of your business is directly related to the effort you can put into it. Poor health or the inability to work hard and long when it's necessary will inevitably slow the growth of your business. Conversely, if you are a very high-energy individual who needs little sleep and seldom gets sick, you can count on putting more than the average effort into your business—and you should reap more than the average reward. All the business owners with whom I've been in contact for the past thirteen years have agreed that we work *much* harder for ourselves than we ever did for another employer—but we enjoy it more and are better rewarded!

■ *Entrepreneurial spirit.* Do risks thrill you or chill you? How long and how hard are you willing to work to realize your dream? Do you measure your success on your own terms or by the values of others? Many of those with the vision of business ownership are true entrepreneurs who get a thrill from the challenge of building a successful business from the ground up. It's equally possible, however, to be successful if you are a "plugger," someone who derives satisfaction from doing the job, day after day, in your own way. To remain in business for a long time requires elements of both personality types—the ability to get started and the ability to keep going.

■ *Juggling skills.* Can you manage multiple projects at the same time? Keep track of numerous clients' needs? Remember to order supplies and pay bills? Schedule client consultations so they don't conflict with family activities? A strong score in this area will be a great assist in productivity and overall business management.

ASSESSING YOUR SKILLS

Although all of the skills mentioned above are necessary for the operation of a desktop publishing business, it is important to note that it is *not* imperative that you possess each and every one yourself. No one is equally skilled in all areas, and what will make your business distinctive is your unique personality and combination of abilities. Still, learning where you are likely to need assistance is important.

Once you have evaluated your individual strengths and weaknesses, you can develop a plan to acquire the additional necessary skills. To establish a well-rounded business, you need to *build on* your existing strengths; *develop* and *improve* areas where you have some skill but not expertise; and finally, *locate* and *utilize* subcontractors, vendors, and other outside services to "fill in the gaps."

Let's take a look at each of these options in more detail.

Build on Your Strengths

Your business will be very much a reflection of yourself—particularly if you are the sole employee. Most likely you are starting the business with specific skills and strengths in a particular area of desktop publishing, whether it be graphics and design, typesetting, or computer wizardry. Additionally, you may have personal characteristics that are particularly well suited to running a service business from your home, such as a positive attitude, a genuine liking for all kinds of people, strong organizational skills, and the ability to manage many tasks at once. Your personal, individual strengths should be the foundation for your business. It does not make sense to start a desktop publishing business with a strong graphic design focus when in fact your skills in this area are rather limited. Similarly, you should be wary about offering writing and proofreading services if you come from a design background and are not particularly skilled in grammar and punctuation.

To focus your business you should first develop a mission statement that outlines your optimum service mix. Examples might be:

- To establish a home-based desktop publishing business that serves corporate clients and specializes in outsourced large projects such as manuals.

- To establish a one-stop desktop publishing service meeting all clients' needs for typesetting, graphic design, and printing and serving primarily small businesses and individuals.

- To integrate desktop publishing with graphic design and to provide services to corporate clients and other DTP businesses.

This mission statement should reflect your ideal ultimate business focus, but it's likely that you will follow a variety of paths toward your goal. You may start out by offering every conceivable service—just to get clients in the door—but, as you become increasingly busy, begin to specialize—*in your area of expertise*—as a way to distinguish your services and to weed out clients who are less desirable *to you*. Having a vision of what you want your business to be will enable you to make decisions based on that ultimate goal. A specific business plan (discussed in chapter 3) will be helpful in focusing your activities. Reviewing your business plan periodically will also help you if you get off track.

For many DTP business owners, focusing their business comes naturally as they promote their services to new and existing clients. Concentrating your advertising and marketing activities in areas relevant to your most desired clients will also effectively screen out a good deal of less desirable work. Additionally, knowing where to get assistance for areas in which you do not wish to specialize will enable you to have these services available to clients without doing the work yourself. (More specific information on working with subcontractors and vendors is presented later in this chapter.)

As you take your business past the start-up stage, you may find that your vision is changing. This is not a problem—after all, it's *your* business! You may discover you don't enjoy certain aspects of the business as much as you thought you would, or you may perceive a potentially very profitable market niche that you would like to pursue. Still, having envisioned a focus for your business will guide you in your decision making; you will be able to make conscious choices with your goal in mind rather than shifting like a weathervane with every change in the wind.

Develop and Improve

While you most likely are not an expert in every facet of desktop publishing, there are no doubt areas in which you feel particularly strong and others in which you have some familiarity but not expertise. Making the effort to increase your skills in these marginal areas will pay dividends in a greater ability to meet your clients' needs. Your skill improvement will also allow you to decrease your reliance on outside experts and expand your business into new and potentially very exciting areas.

For desktop publishers coming from a design background, weak areas might include typesetting and typography or business management skills such as scheduling and record keeping. DTP professionals with a word processing background may be lacking in design skills or a thorough knowledge of printing operations. There are numerous resources for developing skills in the desired areas. The chart below indicates some likely options for a variety of training and education needs.

TRAINING RESOURCES	LOCAL COLLEGE OR UNIVERSITY	COMPUTER USERS' GROUP	PROFESSIONAL ASSOCIATION	SMALL BUSINESS ASSOCIATION	NETWORKING GROUP	BOOKS AND PUBLICATIONS	SEMINARS AND CONFERENCES	INFORMAL NETWORKING	COMPUTER RETAILER	ONLINE RESOURCES
Specific software training	●	●			●	●	●		●	
Graphic design	●		●		●	●				
Typography		●			●	●				
Financial management			●	●		●				
Printing operations						●	●	●		
Computer expertise		●			●	●	●	●	●	●
Marketing			●	●	●	●		●		●

Local college or university. Both credit and noncredit courses are offered by many colleges, including community colleges.

Computer users' group. A computer users' group will frequently offer general overview courses on the computer itself as well as on specific software. These courses are usually reasonably priced, or even free to members, and provide a good foundation that will get you up and running. Local universities may be able to provide information on computer users' groups in your area.

Professional association. Industry-specific professional associations may offer training courses in their field at both beginner and advanced levels. General business organizations such as the Chamber of Commerce or your city's business association may be a good source for business training courses.

Small Business Administration (SBA). This government-sponsored organization provides business assistance in a wide variety of ways, including training courses in small business, helpful publications, and even one-on-one mentoring and advice from seasoned business professionals through SCORE (Service Corps of Retired Executives).

Networking groups are an excellent source of individualized assistance and information. Group members are often willing to share success stories, business strategies, and cautionary tales with other members. Networking groups may be industry-specific or more general. One type of networking group, called a *leads group* or *leads club,* exists solely for the purpose of exchanging business-generating information and referring work to other group members. Becoming active in a networking group may offer great opportunities for learning as well as sharing your own business tips and strategies. You also may hook up with someone who can provide individualized training (such as software training) to meet your specific needs. In a networking group it's important to give as well as receive assistance. For best results, find a group whose members share your general business philosophy and with whom you feel comfortable, to facilitate the exchange of information.

Books and periodicals. Someone, somewhere, has written a book on whatever it is that you need to know! Your local library is an excellent resource for books and periodicals of all kinds. As well, many public libraries belong to interlibrary systems and can obtain books not in their own collections.

You will be wise to locate a bookstore with an excellent business section and visit occasionally just to browse among the titles—you may discover a book that answers questions you haven't even formulated yet. You will also find it valuable to build up a reference library of books pertinent to many facets of your desktop publishing business, including design, typography, marketing and sales, business operations, and grammar and punctuation. A good dictionary and a thesaurus are also essential. Having the right resources at hand when you need them will greatly enhance your productivity and your ability to get the job done right the first time.

Periodicals—magazines and newsletters—are a good source of information on a variety of topics that relate directly to your business, and they also help you to stay current in your field. There are excellent periodicals aimed at the small office–home office market, specific computer system or software users, or the desktop publishing industry in general.

Seminars and conferences on a myriad of topics are presented throughout the year in most major cities. Programs may be offered by hardware or software manufacturers, industry experts, or professional associations. Once your business is on a variety of mailing lists (which will happen rather quickly as soon as you are up and running), you will receive flyers in the mail promoting a variety of learning opportunities. Additionally, professional associations will keep you informed of upcoming events. Typical business seminars provide a half or a full day of information on a specific topic (e.g., training in the new version of PageMaker, the use of color in desktop publishing, assertiveness for women in business). Conferences, more usually two to three days in length, offer a variety of sessions in a number of areas pertinent to members of the sponsoring organization.

Informal networking. As your business develops, you will naturally come in contact with individuals in other, related businesses. These individuals become your informal networking group and are an excellent source of information. For example, by developing a good relationship with a printer you are ensuring you have someone to turn to with a question on printing specifics, so that you can respond knowledgeably to your clients and improve the value of your product. Merely having these resources available to you can increase your confidence to work in areas of desktop publishing that are new to you. Of course, you too will serve as an information source for your network, and this give-and-take promotes close and supportive business partnerships.

Computer retailer. If you are lucky, you will locate a knowledgeable computer retailer who enjoys answering questions and is most concerned with providing you with the system that best meets your needs. On the other hand, you may end up dealing with a high-school-age hacker who speaks condescendingly in a language you don't understand and tries to sell you the newest, fastest, most powerful computer without first ascertaining your needs. Most likely, you will encounter someone who falls somewhere between these two extremes. Many computer stores do provide excellent information, and if you are able to develop a relationship with a good retailer, you will provide yourself with another resource to help you and your clients when you have questions about hardware and software capabilities, new equipment, and the like. If you do make use of such a source for information, it is incumbent upon you to purchase your equipment from the same source—think how you would feel if a potential client took up your valuable time with questions, then took his job down the street to a competitor with less knowledge but lower prices!

Online services. The past few years have witnessed an explosion of online information and communication services, and this resource will continue to expand. Using online services to check for the latest magazine reviews of hardware and software will yield the most current and relevant data. Chat areas devoted to desktop publishing and home-based businesses are often a great source of advice and suggestions, particularly for new businesses. You can benefit from others' experience and enjoy making connections. And there is a good variety of free or low-cost "shareware" available, often unique programs that can meet a specific business need.

Improving your overall business knowledge through this variety of resources is an excellent investment for you to make in your business and will pay off in the long run.

Locate and Utilize Additional Help

It is inevitable that you will at some point take on a project that is beyond your capabilities. Doing so knowing that you have the resources to get the help you need will go a long way toward increasing your confidence—and this will come through to the client. If you speak knowledgeably about using outside sources for specific aspects of the job, the client will know that you understand the complexity of the project and are wise enough to engage an expert for those areas that require it. These outside resources are known as *subcontractors* or *vendors*. (In this book, the words are used interchangeably.)

Subcontractors or vendors are other businesses or individuals to whom you assign a portion or all of a particular project. Vendors' expertise is most often in areas other than your own. Typical vendors for a desktop publishing business include printers, service bureaus, graphic designers, typesetters, couriers, and mailing services. By using appropriate subcontractors, you will benefit in numerous ways. You will be able to expand the range of services you offer to your clients beyond your own areas of expertise. Additionally, the quantity of work you can deliver will be greatly expanded without the cost or hassle of hiring employees. You will maintain control of a project, since work goes to the vendor through you and comes back to you, while you remain the point of contact for the client. You can profit financially by adding an appropriate markup to the vendor's price to you—typical markups in the industry range from 15 to 50 percent. By providing work to the vendor, you are practically guaranteeing yourself a valuable information resource. Additionally, the vendors you use very likely will return the favor, calling on you to perform services related to their own business projects.

Potential downfalls to collaborating with subcontractors include being disappointed with the quality of work and the possibility that the client will choose to work directly with the vendor next time, eliminating your profit and your business relationship with the client. Since you maintain control of the project, you are responsible for the vendor's work being up to the standard expected by the client, and it may be uncomfortable for you to be in the middle between a disgruntled client and a defensive subcontractor. This problem can be avoided, for the most part, by developing positive and ongoing relationships with businesses and individuals whose work is of high quality and who share your commitment to customer satisfaction. A strong collaborative spirit will ensure benefits to all who participate. You also should keep in mind that your primary loyalty is to your client. If a vendor's services are not up to your (or your client's) quality standards, it will be better to discontinue the relationship and locate another subcontractor. In my experience, the occasional less-than-positive experience is far outweighed by the numerous benefits to working with a selection of outstanding vendors.

Develop specific subcontractors whose skills complement yours. A fast, efficient word processing expert is an excellent resource for any desktop publisher. With the assistance of this individual—working on inputting text to a large project while you complete another job, for instance—you can improve your turnaround time by juggling multiple projects simultaneously. In a like manner, assigning a sophisticated logo design to a talented graphic designer, who can deliver the finished job on disk for you to insert into the stationery you create, will quite possibly improve the quality of your work and increase your total billings as well.

Even before you start up your business, you can initiate relationships with potential subcontractors/vendors. If you have not had dealings with a particular service in the past, you will most likely begin with a phone call or brief visit to the vendor's place of business. In your preliminary conversation you should attempt to establish a contact name, the company's charges for the services you envision utilizing, and general policies and procedures. Your goal is to begin a cordial, professional relationship that will ultimately benefit you, the vendor, and the client. Be frank about your knowledge level with the technology involved, and don't be afraid to ask for details about what is included or not included in their prices. Most vendors will be more than pleased to spend a few minutes with you in the interests of establishing a mutually beneficial business relationship.

In this manner, continue to make contact with other services to develop the business alliances you'll need to complement your own skills. (See sample scripts starting on the next page.) Naturally, not every call will be as cordial as those I've scripted. You may encounter obviously incompetent, uninterested, or impolite individuals—people with whom you certainly don't want to pursue a relationship. You will be glad to have made this discovery before attempting to work with them.

You also may approach your subcontractor relationships less formally by setting up arrangements with vendors with whom you are already familiar. Even if you are well known to each other, speak with them specifically about the process of using them as a subcontractor, so

You: Hello, my name is Mary Davis. I'm the president of ABC Desktop Publishing Services, and I'd like to get information on your services so that I can make them available to my clients.

Vendor: Sure, Mary. What can I tell you?

You: First of all, is there a particular individual I should speak with when I call?

Vendor: You can ask for me, Charles. We're a small business, and I sometimes answer the phone as well as doing the bulk of the production work.

You: I can identify with that! I'm basically a one-person business, but I do use subcontractors to meet my clients' extended needs. One need I envision is for high-resolution output. My printer is 600 dpi, but on occasion clients have requested something better. I'm a little unclear on what's available beyond 600. Can you educate me?

Vendor: I'd be glad to. Output from our Linotronics is 1200 or 2400 dpi. We can output to paper or film, positive or negative. We also can produce slides. We work directly from your computer files, given to us either on disk or sent by modem, whichever is more convenient for you.

You: And what are your rates for this service?

The conversation continues. You develop the necessary information and, at the same time, have begun a professional relationship with a helpful and knowledgeable individual—someone who seems pleased to have you as a potential client and is willing to educate you in an area that is new to you.

You: Thank you so much for this information. I'll give you a call when I have a project so we can coordinate the details. Also, I'll send you my brochure and some other information about my company that may be useful if you ever have the need for outside desktop publishing or word processing services.

Vendor: Oh, do you do word processing? Sometimes I have a large project that just needs entering in WP so that I can convert it to DTP. We frequently send out that kind of job.

You: I can certainly help you with that. I'll include my rate sheet in the materials I'm sending. Please give me a call if I can answer any questions for you.

SAMPLE SCRIPT: INITIAL VENDOR CALL (graphic designer)

You: Hello, this is Mary Davis from ABC Desktop Publishing Services. I'm calling to obtain information on your graphic design services.

Vendor: This is Rose McCarthy. I'm the owner of the company and the principal graphic designer. How can I help you?

You: I provide basic design services, but on occasion I have the need for something beyond my capabilities. Do you frequently work with desktop publishers?

Vendor: We have an excellent relationship with three other firms who seem to be in the same circumstance as you. They do all their own typesetting and layout, but when it comes to executing a specific design they're sometimes out of their depth.

You: That's it exactly! I honestly don't know how often I'll be needing to use a graphic designer since my business is new, but it's important to me to have someone available. Would you be willing to meet with me to review some of your work and talk about a business arrangement?

Vendor: I'd like that very much. How about Tuesday at 10:00?

The conversation ends. At the meeting, you review her portfolio and discuss her rates. It's a good idea for you to have specific design challenges in mind and get from her a price range for that type of project. Before concluding your conversation with her, be sure to remind her that you are available to do the desktop publishing for any projects for which she or other clients have a need.

that they understand what your needs will be. An additional source of subcontractors may be a networking group of business owners in desktop publishing and related fields.

Another way to locate subcontractors for a specific type of work is to run a "help wanted" ad in your local newspaper. I have had great success finding word processors through this method. (The Internal Revenue Service has specific guidelines distinguishing subcontractors from employees, and you should review these to be sure you are not entering into an employer-employee relationship.)

Having the necessary vendors in place *before* you need them will make the process run much more smoothly when you do have occasion to use an outside service.

Excellent services to subcontract are those that are not profitable for you to provide. These might include such things as courier/delivery service, word processing, or mailing services. It is very likely you will need these services from time to time in your business, but it may not be worth your while to do these tasks yourself. For example:

- A client requests that you rush his proof over to him as soon as it's finished so that he can share it at a board meeting that afternoon. By utilizing a courier service, you save your own valuable time and merely add the delivery charge (plus appropriate markup) to the client's bill.

- One of your best clients starts graduate school and asks you to word process her term papers. The typical word processing rate in your town is $24 an hour, and you are currently booked to capacity with desktop design work at $65 an hour. You locate a word processing service that will complete the work for you with a rapid turnaround. You pass along the cost to your client with only a modest markup for your liaison services, considering it a service to an excellent client that will pay off in good will in the long run—and you save yourself from getting bogged down with low-paying, rush-basis word processing.

- After completing the design of a brochure, you are requested by your client to handle printing and mailing of the brochure to 500 of his customers. You subcontract the printing and oversee the delivery of the finished brochures to a secretarial business that performs bulk-mailing services. Your client is delighted because he is able to pay bulk-mail rates without securing his own permit, and the secretarial service is pleased to have the job of preparing the mailing. Your billing to your client includes your own design time, plus time to manage the different parts of the whole process. Additionally, you add a fair markup to both the printer's and the secretarial service's invoices—thus significantly increasing your total billing to this client while minimizing your own involvement in work outside your area of expertise.

In your initial contact with a subcontractor, you should have discussed in general terms how you envision working together. When establishing rates, be sure to talk about any discounts either of you may offer—with some businesses a professional discount is applied when the work is being done for a third party (your client). If this is the case, you will be expected to extend a similar discount to your vendors for work done for their clients. You may find that projects done for knowledgeable vendors are very profitable for you. In most cases the information given to you is complete and well organized, and your assignment is quite specific. You are dealing with people who have an excellent knowledge of the capabilities of desktop publishing, and you will rapidly develop a smooth working relationship; therefore, the time you might typically allot for client discussions, explanations, review of work, and the like may be significantly less than standard. As a result of these factors, you may feel that a vendor discount is justified and is, in fact, an excellent investment in your ongoing relationship.

When subcontracting your own work to a vendor, go over your expectations again when you first discuss a particular project. Be very specific about deadlines and anticipated outcomes. Using a consistent Subcontractor Job Summary will reduce the chance of any misunderstandings. Request billing at the time the job is delivered so you can immediately apply the charges to your client's invoice.

Following are sample Subcontractor Job Summaries—one blank form and two filled in for services related to a hypothetical newsletter project. These Job Summaries cover the subcontracting of two elements of the production of the newsletter: text entry of the major articles by a word processing specialist, and printing of the final, approved newsletter. When filling out the Job Summary, provide relevant details to the subcontractors. In some instances, of course, specifications would be much more detailed, and for the most part, any subcontracting assignment would be preceded by a conversation with the subcontractor discussing details of the job. So the information provided is merely a reminder of the job specifications already understood by the subcontractor. Job Summaries are returned by the subcontractor on completion of the job to provide billing information and other details, and a copy is kept in the client's file with the final invoice. (More detailed information on organizing work, establishing priorities, tracking projects, and billing is provided in chapter 6.)

professional desktop
publishing services

LOUISE M. KURSMARK

9847 Catalpa Woods Court
Cincinnati, Ohio 45242

513-792-0030

SUBCONTRACTOR JOB SUMMARY

Date in _____

Client _____

Job _____

_____

_____

_____

Subcontractor / date assigned _____

Estimated time to complete _____

Special instructions _____

_____

_____

_____

_____

_____

_____

Due back to Best Impression _____ Due to client _____

BILLING SUMMARY

Date _____ Service _____ Hours _____ Charge _____

Date _____ Service _____ Hours _____ Charge _____

Date _____ Service _____ Hours _____ Charge _____

Please attach relevant supporting materials.

professional desktop
publishing services

LOUISE M. KURSMARK

9847 Catalpa Woods Court
Cincinnati, Ohio 45242

513-792-0030

SUBCONTRACTOR JOB SUMMARY

Date in _____12/1/95_____

Client _____Mullins Real Estate_____

Job _____Newsletter copy: 5 articles_____

_____

_____

_____

Subcontractor/date assigned _____Mary Douglas, 12/4/95_____

Estimated time to complete _____2-2.5 hours_____

Special instructions _____Each article a separate file._____

_____Set titles in upper/lower case, not all caps as written._____

_____

5 articles: RE News   4th Qtr sales

              Pres. Column   Und. Escrow

              Emp. Spotlight

Due back to Best Impression _____12/7 a.m._____   Due to client _____12/11_____

BILLING SUMMARY

Date ___12/5___ Service ___word processing___ Hours _2.2_ Charge _$52.80_

Date ___12/6___ Service ___delivery___ Hours _____ Charge _$5.00_

Date _____ Service _____ Hours _____ Charge _____

Please attach relevant supporting materials.

SUBCONTRACTOR JOB SUMMARY

Date in _____ 12/1/95 _____

Client _____ Mullins Real Estate _____

Job _____ 8-page newsletter _____

Subcontractor/date assigned _____ CopyCat, 12/12/95 _____

Estimated time to complete _____

Special instructions _____ qty.: 500 _____

See last issue (copy attached) for paper, colors, etc.

Screens on pages 3, 5, 7, 8.

Laser proof provided with color marked.

Film negatives will be delivered to you today by Pro-Graphics.

Due back to Best Impression _____ 12/18 _____ Due to client _____ Deliv. 12/19 a.m. _____

BILLING SUMMARY

Date _____ 12/18 _____ Service _____ Detailed invoice attached _____ Hours _____ Charge $453.50

Date _____ Service _____ Hours _____ Charge _____

Date _____ Service _____ Hours _____ Charge _____

Please attach relevant supporting materials.

...ay feel it is more beneficial to refer callers direct-
...e specialized area may be totally outside your own
...you may be over your head already in overdue pro-
...ents. In these cases you may confidently refer callers
...ors, knowing that they will provide the necessary ser-
...on, remember the referral and return the favor when

...ster of reliable vendors also ensures that you won't have
to turn work away because you're already booked to capacity. Instead, you
can subcontract out some or all of a project, even services you would normally provide yourself (for example, basic desktop publishing). The dual
advantage is that you keep the client and the client receives a reasonable
turnaround time.

One additional benefit to working with vendors that may not be
apparent at first is that by developing these relationships, you create for
yourself a collaborative work environment that can keep you from feeling
isolated and alone in your business venture. It's almost like having co-
workers—people with whom you can joke, share the work, commiserate
about work problems, and enjoy an insider status. I consider my vendor
relationships to be one of the definite benefits of operating my own business! My experiences have been nearly all positive and have resulted in a
greatly improved level of service to my clients.

As noted earlier in this chapter, it is not necessary that you yourself
have every skill and qualification required to operate a professional desktop publishing business. Instead, the combination of your own unique
talents and the resources of other businesses and individuals will allow
you to provide complete services to meet your clients' diverse needs. The
secret to your success will be knowing and capitalizing on your strengths
while locating other services to complement your abilities.

SUBCONTRACTOR EXPERIENCES

DESKTOP PUBLISHERS

Doug Wilcox, WordSmith, Rockland, Massachusetts: "Subcontracting allows me to get extra work done at good profit margins without the expense of hiring. I wish I could find a good desktop publisher to subcontract to."

Anna Callwood, Bac-Up Business Services, Boston, Massachusetts: "I think the best way to deal with a subcontractor is to discuss what you want and what they expect, and establish a mutual project work-out/timeframe, etc."

Mick O'Grady, Park Avenue Secretarial Service, Dayton, Ohio: "I've found a great resource in my quick print shop—his prepress operator takes care of all stripping for me, adjusts the layout for the press, etc."

VENDORS

Roseanne DiSanto, DiSanto Design, Boston, Massachusetts: "Idealistically, I am looking for a partnership—someone with a good sense of design who can take my rough layouts and make them even better. Someone who has an incredible eye for how things are placed on a page and pays attention to every single detail in a layout. Someone who also knows the finer points of pre-production and who can translate a layout into a file format that a printer can read. Someone who will take the initiative to get to know my clients and my work style, and who can then make some valuable contributions to my business."

Keith Killian, North Shore Printing, North Reading, Massachusetts: "Printers and DTP professionals can learn a lot from each other. We're seeing more work come in to us on disk, and we foresee huge advances in the printing industry that will require us to be more knowledgeable about desktop publishing. We're happy to share our expertise, and in return we look to our desktop publishing sources for information when we need it."

CHAPTER THREE

PLANNING FOR SUCCESS

> Well begun is half done. — **PROVERBS**

efore actually opening for business, you will make important decisions about the services you'll offer, the prices you'll charge, and what you will name your business. Other critical preopening responsibilities include reviewing legal and zoning issues, analyzing the competition, determining your equipment needs and financing options, and writing a business plan. In this chapter we'll discuss all these considerations and how your planning now will provide a firm foundation for your business's success.

GATHERING INFORMATION

As recommended in the previous chapter, you should utilize books, magazines, newsletters, and organizations to increase your knowledge on a variety of topics related to your business. The Appendix provides complete contact information for numerous sources. Now, while your business is in the planning and start-up stages, is the time to review the various publications available and select those that seem most relevant and useful. Joining professional organizations will expose you to the latest trends in your field as well as provide opportunities to purchase books, attend conventions, and tap into resources that will be of great help as your business grows.

Networking groups and professional organizations often provide good insight into publications that will be of value. In some cases, you can let group members do the prescreening for you. In my own experience, after hearing raves about *Home Office Computing* from several members of my networking group, I was convinced to subscribe and have found this magazine to be a valuable resource—and probably not one I would have picked up otherwise.

With all the reading and learning you'll be doing, it will be impossible to retain all the information. You may even read articles or skim books on topics that seem to have no immediate relevance to your business. This is very natural, due to the "information overload" you'll likely be experiencing. It is important, however, that you provide yourself with opportunities for learning, make note of publications that might be of value in the future, and expose yourself to new technologies and trends that will likely be extremely relevant down the road. Keeping informed and aware is essential for your business. At a later time, when a client or vendor refers to some new technique or capability, you will at least have a vague idea of what he or she is talking about and be able to respond intelligently. At the very least you can say, "Yes, I remember reading about that in last month's *MacUser* magazine. Tell me how you're using it."

Keeping up to speed in a field as constantly changing as desktop publishing is a challenge, but it is a business necessity. Developing good resources—books, magazines, newsletters, organizations, and individuals—will help keep you on top of what's new and how it affects your clients and your business.

NAMING YOUR BUSINESS

When deciding what to name your business, there are several important factors to consider:

- *How does it sound?* Is it easy to pronounce? Is it memorable?
- *What does it say about your business*—and is that the image you want to portray? "Dollar-Saver Desktop Publishing" is fine if you want to be

known for your low prices; "Debbie's Desktop Designs" may be too cute to appeal to a corporate market; "Professional Business Graphics" is not the best choice if you also want to attract word processing clients.

- *Does it limit you or indicate an inaccurate specialization?* "Page Makers" as a business name will probably eliminate clients who would like you to use Quark. I once knew of a real estate company called "Christian Homes" that used a cross as its logo; I wondered if they refused to work for non-Christian clients (thus severely limiting their market).

- *Is it positioned near the beginning of the alphabet?* Though much desktop publishing work is gained through sources other than Yellow Pages advertising, you definitely give yourself an edge in these directories by being listed near the top of your category. I proved this to myself, indisputably, when I changed my name from one beginning with *S* to one beginning with *B* and, running the same ad under "Resumes" in my local Yellow Pages, increased my resume business 59 percent and achieved a substantial increase in new calls. (Chapter 5 contains more information about Yellow Pages advertising and the benefits of being listed in multiple categories.)

In choosing a name, consider words that are descriptive of what you do and evocative of the spirit you wish your business to portray (words such as *quality, professional, graphic, creative, compelling, A-1,* and *fine*). You might feel comfortable using your name (*Amelia Smith Associates* or *Daniels Design*), particularly if it positions you at the front of the alphabet.

My own business name started out, way back in 1982, as *Secretarial Services Unlimited.* Obviously I did not follow my own guidelines! The name is difficult to say, not memorable, indicates a specialization that was soon outdated, and began with a letter toward the end of the alphabet. I was able to launch a successful business in spite of its name, but there is no need for you to work quite so hard! After ten years in business, six of them in desktop publishing, I decided to change my business name and became *Best Impression.* The new name indicates a broader focus, is easy to pronounce, gives an impression of high quality, and is a *B*—and the results were all I had hoped for in terms of positive client reaction and increased business.

When you have come up with two or three names that appeal to you and fit the criteria above, try them out with friends and family. Ask them for their immediate reaction to each proposed name. Design preliminary logos for a few names and see if that advances your thought process. Once you have established a "look" for your business via letterhead, business cards, logo, brochures, and advertising, it may be difficult and counterproductive to change your business name. So select it carefully.

When you are down to a few finalists, do a name check in local telephone directories and with the Secretary of State's office to be sure there are no duplicates in your locality.

LEGAL AND REGULATORY ISSUES

Once you've determined to start a home-based business, you will need to explore *zoning* and *business registration* issues. States, towns, and cities all have their own regulations. A simple phone call to your town or city clerk can usually yield the answer to the question, How do I register my home-based business? In Massachusetts, in two towns where I established my business, I filled out a simple form at the town clerk's office, paid a modest fee (in the $20 to $40 range), and was in business. (This is sometimes known as a DBA—Doing Business As—Certificate.) When relocating my business to Ohio, I learned that I had to file a registration certificate with the Secretary of State's office for statewide registration. I also had to register my business name and be assured that it did not duplicate another name already on file. In Massachusetts, only corporations need to register on a statewide basis.

Zoning requirements, which establish the activities that may be conducted at a specific address, vary tremendously from town to town. Some business owners I know have had to go through a significant bureaucratic process (public hearings before the Zoning Board, notice to abuttors, etc.) in order to operate a home-based business. To obtain the most recent and accurate information, check with your town or city to determine the regulations that apply in your individual locality. Be proactive in finding out the zoning-approval process so that you can head off potential problems by gathering traffic information, neighbor approvals, a history of typical activities in similar businesses, and information on home businesses in general. If you are called upon to appear before the

Zoning Board, you will have facts and figures at your fingertips and will be able to speak knowledgeably and confidently.

Your town's zoning regulations regarding home-based businesses may include restrictions on the number of visits per day by customers and suppliers; whether a business sign is permitted and, if so, its size and overall appearance; the portion of your home that can be used for business; and the type of equipment that is allowed. If your town is overly restrictive about these issues, you might consider leading an effort to have the rules changed. Home-based businesses are becoming increasingly common. In particular, the number of professional businesses located in residences has increased enormously in the past ten years. It is understandable that a town would want to restrict customer traffic or retail operations, but the corporate world has changed significantly, and in many instances towns and cities have not yet caught up. (*Home Office Computing* magazine conducts an annual study of the best places in the United States to operate a home-based business. If you have the flexibility to move before you begin your business, check the latest study for appealing locations.)

Once you are registered with your city or town, you will be required to pay *personal property tax* (usually a modest amount) on your business equipment. Typically, you will receive a form in the mail yearly, asking you to list your equipment and its value. You may also be visited once a year by city assessors, who will review your office setup to ensure that it is consistent with the reports you have filed.

Individual states also have their own rules regarding the collection of *sales tax* by desktop publishers. It is your responsibility to determine and comply with the requirements in your state. If you are required to collect sales tax, most often you will submit payments and a report quarterly. Check your state's requirements and establish your own internal procedure for compliance.

STRUCTURING YOUR BUSINESS

There are advantages and disadvantages to each form of business organization—sole proprietorship, partnership, corporation, and limited-liability company. Let's briefly examine each type of business structure and its pros and cons.

- *Sole proprietorship.* This is the simplest form of business ownership and the least expensive to establish. Basically, you declare yourself in business and merely have to comply with the business registration requirements in your locality, as described in the previous section. You are personally responsible for the debts of the business, and you are entitled to all the profits—on which you pay personal income tax, completing a Schedule C, Business Profit or Loss, and attaching it to your federal and state income tax returns. Most small and home-based businesses start out as sole proprietorships; some restructure into corporations when they experience significant growth, take on employees, and in general require a more complex business organization. Sole proprietors may experience difficulty raising money unless they provide personal collateral.

- *Partnership.* This, obviously, involves two or more people, so if you are a one-person business you need not consider this structure. A partnership agreement, detailing the ownership share, rights and obligations of each partner, and many other details, should be prepared by a lawyer. Particularly important to include are clauses concerning what happens when either partner wishes to dissolve the partnership. For tax purposes, each partner completes a Schedule K-1 listing their partnership tax liability for that year and includes it with their personal income tax return. Raising money for a partnership may also be difficult, and, again, personal collateral may be required by the lending institution.

- *Corporation.* The Subchapter-S Corporation, intended for small businesses, provides the shareholders-owners with some tax advantages and limits of liability (that is, you are not personally responsible for the debts of the business). Forming a corporation requires complex document preparation (usually requiring an attorney), which can be expensive, as well as annual filing and reporting and their associated costs. Raising money is generally simpler for a corporation than for a sole proprietorship or partnership.

- *Limited-Liability Company* or *Limited-Liability Partnership.* These two new types of business organization, not yet available in every state, offer the advantages of corporations and partnerships (limited liability) without the disadvantages (higher taxes).

Although it is likely you will begin your business as a sole proprietorship, part of your overall business knowledge should be a general understanding of the types of business structures available and the advantages and disadvantages of each. It is advisable to consult an attorney or business expert if you have questions about business structure or decide to pursue a partnership or corporation.

In the course of operating my business, I have not had occasion to require the services of an attorney. I have used an accountant to prepare my tax returns but not for day-to-day business advice. You may wish to utilize the services of either or both of these professionals. Making contacts when you are setting up your business makes sense; you can benefit from their advice and establish a business relationship to call upon when the need arises.

ANALYZING YOUR COMPETITORS

Getting a handle on your competition is a must! This information will help you as you define and refine your business strategies, service offerings, prices, and policies. If, for example, you find that every other desktop publisher in your area offers two-day standard turnaround, you will find yourself at a disadvantage if you plan to complete routine jobs within a week. On the other hand, if you learn that other services charge separately for proofreading, you may want to include this service in your project quotes without breaking out the cost as an extra. You may choose to do what other services are doing, or *not* to do what they are doing. The choice is yours, but having the knowledge will make your choice an informed one.

Your first task is to identify your desktop publishing competition. Start by examining *Yellow Pages directories* for your immediate area and surrounding areas. Look under every possible category that relates to desktop publishing—such as typesetting, printing, graphic design, word processing/typing/secretarial services, and computer services—as well as the desktop publishing category itself. Not all businesses advertise in the Yellow Pages, of course. Try to obtain the *membership directories* of professional and civic organizations. (If you become a member, in most cases you will receive a directory, but you may be able to obtain one merely by calling the organization.) Ask your *vendors and subcontractors* what other desktop publishing businesses they are familiar with. If a *regional business newspaper* or journal is available in your area, scan the pages for desktop publishing services' ads. Many DTP firms, especially if they are small, will not advertise in large metropolitan daily papers, but small-town or *weekly papers* would be another good place to check for competitors' ads.

As you start developing names of competing businesses, create a master list that you can update as necessary. Include business name, address, phone number, and contact name, if you have one. You might break the list down into subcategories of direct and less-direct competitors, or local and distant competitors. The purpose of the list is for you to track competitor information easily, so organize it in any way that makes sense to you. Your next step is to complete your list with specific information about each competitor.

One of the easiest ways to learn about your competitors is to pose as a potential client and make a telephone inquiry. Have in mind a specific project to discuss so that you can ask questions naturally and respond to their queries. Learn as much as you can about their hourly rates, turnaround time, standard policies, and overall business philosophy. To be fair, don't prolong the conversation or promise to bring work in. Fill in the details on your master list, and be prepared to track and review this information every six months to a year, to find out who is still in business, whose rates have gone up, and other pertinent information.

In a networking or professional group, you will have the opportunity to meet and talk with competing business owners. In the true spirit of networking, much business information will be shared freely, although many businesses are leery about sharing rates or profitability details. Once you have established contact with other business owners, you may feel comfortable calling them occasionally to ask about general business information.

Now, armed with this competitive information, you are ready to examine your specific market for opportunities for your own business.

SELECTING YOUR SERVICE MIX/ IDENTIFYING NICHES

Having a general idea of the prices and services prevalent in your area will give you a snapshot of the desktop publishing marketplace. Use this information to select services and identify market niches where you can stand out. The idea is to exploit your own unique areas of expertise to take advantage of the opportunities you discover as a result of your research.

Here are some specific focus areas you may wish to consider:

- *Graphic design.* If your area is loaded with competent desktop publishers who seem somewhat lacking in design skills, or with great graphic designers who still work on an old-fashioned pasteboard, the combination of graphic design with skilled desktop publishing may be a profitable and successful market niche.

- *Typography and layout.* If you have a real eye for the details of type and the overall look of page layout, along with outstanding grammar, spelling, and proofreading skills, you can bill this as your particular strength. You may even be able to subcontract work from other DTP services or graphic designers who would like to take advantage of your skills in this area.

- *Fast service.* Particularly for new services with lots of time and relatively few clients, providing speedy turnaround may be an excellent entree into a crowded market. You will need to advertise and promote this facet of your business—and, critically, you will need to deliver on your promise.

- *Low rates.* This is a tricky area to target, since with low rates profitability depends upon volume and, if you are a one-person business, your volume is limited by the number of hours you can work. You might, however, consider offering discounted rates to other DTP services, ad agencies, graphic designers, and other professionals, while keeping your normal prices for the general public. This will enable you to gain experience at a highly professional level while not locking you in as the "bargain basement" service. As business improves and your general client base expands, you may then raise your rates to your professional clients or gradually phase out of working for them.

- *Technical expertise.* Perhaps your particular skill lies in a thorough understanding of the most advanced facets of DTP technology. Working with color, scanning and manipulating complex graphics, incorporating photographs, preparing multimedia presentations—

these are all areas that are at the high end of technological services. With skills in these areas, you may wish to offer yourself as an expert to other desktop publishers as well as to regular business clients.

- *Large-project specialist.* If your forte is handling large and complex projects, you will be a valuable resource for companies faced with these major challenges to their normal work flow. A potential downfall to this specialization is that you may become dependent on one company or one project for the bulk of your business, and when this dries up (which may happen for a variety of reasons), you will have little to fall back upon. An advantage is that one large project provides significant work for a lengthy period of time.

- *Small-business specialist.* Since desktop publishing services can be used by virtually every business, there are opportunities to specialize away from corporate clients and toward "Main Street" retailers and small businesses. If you enjoy working directly with business owners, being perceived as the expert in every area relating to document production, and providing relatively small-scale services, you will enjoy this niche. Examples of products used by small businesses include retailer price lists and sale flyers, business forms and invoices, stationery and business cards, and menus. An advantage to this particular category is the large number of potential clients; disadvantages may be the relatively small budget with which many clients will be working and the limited scope for advanced graphic design talents.

Determining your likely client profile will help you plan your advertising and marketing efforts, business policies, and rates. Once you have in mind the target market for your services, you are ready to develop a list of service offerings and rates. It is wise to complete this list before you begin business so that you sound prepared and professional when greeting your first potential client. Of course, you are free to change any of this information at any time it seems necessary or desirable. Nothing you do in the planning stages is cast in stone; your plans are merely guidelines and foundations for your future business.

When developing your service offerings, start by being as comprehensive as possible. List every type of service you can think of that a client might require from a desktop publishing service. Then categorize your list by those services you yourself wish to perform and those for which you will need to locate outside sources (vendors/subcontractors, as discussed in chapter 2).

The sample chart on the following page offers a good starting point. I've provided a blank, for your use, and a filled-in version as an example.

In this hypothetical example, I've elected to provide desktop publishing, word processing, scanning, and limited graphic design services, plus laser printing, low-volume copying, and faxing. I've also located sources for two types of graphic design (by hand and on computer); two types of printing (quick and commercial); slide, color, and high-resolution output; supplemental word processing; mailing services; and complex scanning. This package of service offerings draws upon my own skills and strengths while providing the resources to meet my clients' needs for complete desktop publishing and design.

Your chart should reflect your unique abilities and also show that you have the resources available to complement your skills. At this stage in your planning, it's important to start thinking about how and where you will obtain the additional services that you may be called upon to provide. (Refer to chapter 2 for guidelines and sample scripts for establishing cooperative vendor/subcontractor relationships.) You will feel much more comfortable discussing, for example, color output in regard to a client's specific project when you know where you can get it, how long it will take, and how much it will cost.

DETERMINING YOUR START-UP NEEDS

Operating a professional desktop publishing service requires certain basic equipment and supplies. In this section we'll look at the essentials as well as some add-ons you may want to consider—and how necessary you can expect them to be. An estimated price range is also given, to assist you with planning.

Computer Equipment

Whether you use an *IBM-compatible* or a *Macintosh* computer is up to you. PageMaker, the software that ushered in the desktop publishing revolution, was first created for the Macintosh and its graphical user interface

SERVICE	ME ✔	RATE	OTHER PROVIDER, RATE	NOTES

(Rates given are hypothetical and may not be applicable for your business or geographic area.)

SERVICE	ME ✔	RATE	OTHER PROVIDER, RATE	NOTES
Desktop publishing	✔	$48/hr.	ABC DTP, $40/hr.	Courtesy discount; I will charge the same rate when doing work for ABC
Word processing	✔	$24/hr.	Mary Douglas, independent, $12/hr.	Available weekends
			Word Pro Secretarial Service, $25/hr.	Overnight service available for 25% add'l.
Scanning	✔	$20/scan	Pro-Graphics, color photograph & other complex scans, $25/scan	Rates do not include clean-up
Photocopying	✔	12¢/page	CopyCat, low as 3¢ for volume copying	Contact: Dale
Laser printing	✔	$1/page		
Color prints	✔	$4/page	Pro-Graphics, dye-sub $9/page, posters, etc.	
Slides			Pro-Graphics, $8/slide	
Offset Printing			CopyCat—spot color printing/quick printer	
			JP Printing—process color/commercial printer	Work with Jim on pre-press requirements
High-resolution output			Pro-Graphics: Linotronic $10/page; negs $15	Check for multi-page pricing before submitting
			OutHouse: volume discounts	Contact: Anne
Fax	✔	$2/page		No charge faxing to/from clients
Mailing services			Stellar Business Services; check each time for price	Clients can use Stellar's bulk mail permit for $15 yearly fee. Postage must be paid up front.
Graphic design	✔	$60/hr.	Dell Design, $90/hr.	Michael Dell. Provides hand-drawn graphics; I'll then scan and utilize.
			The Design Center, $120/hr.	On disk. High quality and ready to import.

(GUI). In the years since, however, IBM has pretty much caught up with Mac in all relevant areas, and the choice is one of personal preference. (One exception is the relatively new—and growing—area of multimedia, where the Mac still holds a decided advantage.)

The Mac tends to be easier to use and set up, and its software is easier to install; it also has greater compatibility among software and extensions and greater similarity across programs. The IBM has a reputation for being less expensive and having more widely available peripherals and software. Macs are preferred by many graphic designers and experienced desktop publishers—including me! My first computer was a Macintosh, and I've never owned any other kind, though I've had occasion to utilize others' IBM-compatibles. If you are unfamiliar with either type of computer, or are equally familiar with both, it's my opinion that the Mac is a better choice because chores such as setup and software installation are simpler—thus reducing one of many small-business owners' biggest headaches—and the similarity among different programs makes learning new software a bit easier. Additionally, the Mac has done a good job of making it possible to read and use IBM files; in fact, the latest Macintosh computers can work directly in both Macintosh and DOS/Windows environments. If you are an experienced IBM user, however, it makes sense to stick with the platform you know. As well, the introduction of Windows '95 has brought some formerly Mac-only features to the IBM world, so the distinctions between the two platforms continue to narrow.

Another factor to consider when making your choice of computer platform is the capabilities of the various service bureaus in your area. Since you'll probably need to use these businesses for film, color separations, or other specialty outputs, you should assure yourself that they can work with the files you'll be using. While Macintosh-based service bureaus are more prevalent, there are many that specialize in IBM or handle both types of files. Find out what's available in your area. Using an incompatible service bureau (even with file conversion capabilities) is likely to cause font conflicts and other headaches—just what you *don't* need. So check around before making a final decision on Mac or IBM.

It's likely that at some point you will purchase a second computer for your business, to use as a spare or backup, to accommodate occasional freelancers, or to enable you to work on two projects simultaneously. At that time you can assess whether it makes sense to duplicate your primary computer setup or whether you should cross platforms to expand your business's computer capabilities.

Whatever computer you buy, you will be wise to get the most you can afford in terms of *RAM* (Random Access Memory—the memory with which the computer works to run software) and *hard-disk capacity* (for storage of software and documents). Software is in a continual state of improvement, and with each upgrade comes the need for more memory. Desktop-published documents, particularly those containing graphics, tend to be significantly larger than those created with other types of applications, such as word processors or spreadsheets. Working with photographs and other complex images is particularly memory-intensive. Having insufficient memory or storage space will slow you down considerably and be a daily annoyance and productivity waster.

Desktop publishers require a larger-than-standard *computer monitor.* While it's possible to get by with a standard 14- or 15-inch monitor, you will be amazed at the difference a larger monitor (17, 19 or 20 inches) will make. Putting your money into a faster computer and a larger monitor is a sound investment in those specific items that will most affect your daily work life.

An *extended keyboard* and a comfortable *mouse* are other essentials. These two items will soon feel like an extension of your hands, so it's vital that they be comfortable and reliable.

Another significant expense is *software.* Your basic requirements include professional *desktop publishing* software (most likely PageMaker, Quark, or Corel), other *graphics* capabilities (such as image editing and manipulation, drawing, scanning), an ample *font* selection, and *word processing.* Additional software purchases may include a *presentation program, spreadsheet, business finance package, optical character recognition* (OCR) software (enabling you to edit and utilize scanned text), *database,* and numerous other specific software packages designed to perform a wide array of functions. New and enhanced software is introduced daily, and keeping on top of all of this information can be a daunting task!

Computer and business magazines are a great help in evaluating available software packages based on their tests of competing programs. One of your business startup activities will be to research the latest reviews of a specific type of software you are considering. Check the index of computer magazines such as *MacWorld* or *PC Week* to find out when they last tested PageMaker, Quark, and their competitors, for example. Read the latest reviews and determine which program best suits your anticipated needs. If you have Internet access, you can obtain a great deal of information at numerous online sites, and it will be the most current data available.

Recently, inexpensive desktop publishing software has come on the scene. Although these programs offer numerous features and capabilities at very attractive prices (in some cases, under $100), I caution against buying one of them as your primary desktop publishing program. Since you are planning to run a business specializing in DTP, you should buy the tool most capable of meeting your needs now *and* in the future. As you become more and more expert at desktop publishing and your clients come to expect increasingly sophisticated and complex work, you will find yourself bumping up against the limits of these low-end programs. It makes sense to start out with the most powerful program available in your chosen field to give yourself some growing room and provide the capabilities for future as well as present expertise.

There are other areas, however, where you can save. It's not essential to get the most expensive, full-featured software program for every one of your applications. For instance, if you are planning to use a database only to manage your own client list, you may find yourself perfectly satisfied with an inexpensive, minimum-featured database program, or you might even use your word processing software for this purpose. In this instance, you would be wise to save your software dollars for a program that will more directly affect your area of primary expertise—and thus your bottom line.

When shopping for computers, get complete information on any software that comes "bundled" with the system. Often a computer retailer will put together a "desktop publishing package" that includes increased computer speed and memory, a larger monitor, and specific DTP-related software. This may be a very good buy if it includes the essentials you're looking for. Another alternative is to purchase a software "suite"—a compatible selection of software by one manufacturer. Lotus and Microsoft are two large companies that produce suites. For a very good price you get a number of complete programs. Check the prices on each of the individual programs you're buying and see if a suite makes more sense, even if you don't plan on using all the software that's included.

A high-quality *laser printer* is your next item for consideration. As of the time this book is being written, 600 dpi (dots per inch) is the standard for laser printers. Printers with 300 dpi are still being sold, but their output is not of sufficiently high quality for a desktop publishing service. Don't compromise the quality of your work by printing it on a less-than-adequate printer. To print the highest-quality fonts and graphics, a PostScript printer is required. (PostScript is a printer language that enables better reproduction of fonts and graphics.) PostScript printers are more expensive than non-PostScript. Some non-PostScript printers will emulate PostScript output, but, again, you may find your options for future growth limited with a lower-end printer.

It is advisable for you to have a *color printer*—if only because they are becoming more commonly found in the business world. As a professional in your field, you need to stay at the head of the pack with regard to graphic capabilities. Having a color printer enables you to make available to your clients color overhead transparencies, graphics, report covers, charts and graphs, and other small-quantity jobs for which the cost of color offset printing would be prohibitive. You can also produce color proofs that fully and accurately portray your designs to clients before proceeding to the printing press. If finances prevent you from starting out with a color printer, put it near the top of your list for future acquisitions. The prices of color printers continue to drop while capabilities and quality improve, so be sure to do a careful review of currently available printers when you are ready to make your purchase.

A *scanner* is rapidly becoming a necessity, though you may be able to get along without one initially. Scanners enable you to convert work on paper (drawings, photographs, client logos, etc.) into graphics usable by your computer system. Old-fashioned cut-and-paste methods can certainly be used (and, in fact, it may be more efficient and cost-effective to use them on some projects), but scanning graphics into the computer enables you to resize and edit them, allowing for greater functionality and inclusion into various documents. You may also scan text, but unless you utilize *OCR* (optical character recognition) software, the text will remain as a graphic and you will not be able to edit it. OCR software is useful for inputting pages of cleanly typed text, saving considerable retyping. In many cases, though, unless the quality of the material is very high, scanning and then cleaning up the resulting scan may take longer than retyping the material. Frequently, the purchase of a scanner includes limited OCR software, and if you experiment with this and find that you are using it extensively, it may then be worthwhile to trade up to the full-featured OCR program.

Whether or not you're an experienced driver on the information superhighway, you will need a *modem*. Get the highest speed available, as this technology, too, is being frequently improved. Modems, which are inexpensive and simple to operate, are used to transfer information from your computer to another computer over telephone lines. Joining one of the popular online services, such as America Online, Prodigy, or Compuserve, is an easy way to gain e-mail capabilities along with information and services available to online subscribers and access to the vast Internet and World Wide Web sites. A modem is the most efficient way to transfer your files to a service bureau for output in high-resolution, negative, oversized print, or slide format. Many service bureaus have their own modem-communication programs and will assist you in getting set up to use them. Savvy clients with modems of their own may request that you transfer files to them electronically. Modems are fast becoming standard business equipment.

Additional computer-related equipment you will want to consider includes:

- A *disk backup* system—it's an absolute necessity that you back up your files in some fashion. (See chapter 6 for suggestions on backup routines.)

- A *virus protection* program—a *must* if you *ever* intend to accept a floppy disk from a client or other source or download software from online sources. A computer virus can completely cripple your system. It's just not worth the risk when virus protection is so cheap, easy to use, and effective.

- *File compression* software—to make your DTP documents smaller for transmitting to a service bureau and to save space on your hard drive and backup system. These programs, too, are inexpensive and easy to use.

- A *CD-ROM*—typically included with newer computers; useful for accessing large volumes of clip art and fonts and simplifying the installation of large programs. Also, Kodak's Photo CD allows you to

START-UP ESTIMATES

COMPUTER EQUIPMENT

ITEM	PRICE RANGE
Computer system, monitor, keyboard, mouse, hard drive, CD-ROM, modem	$3,500–$7,000
Laser printer (min. 600 dpi, PostScript)	$1,800–$2,500
Backup system	$250–$800
Scanner	$400–$2,000
Color printer	$800–$2,500
TOTAL: Computer Equipment	$6,750–$14,800

SOFTWARE

ITEM	PRICE RANGE
Page layout	$500–$800
Word processing	$200–$350
Graphics/drawing program	$250–$350
Presentation program	$200–$300
Spreadsheet, database, financial mgmt., misc.	$250–$550
Fonts	$200–$500
Clip art	$100–$400
TOTAL: Software	$1,700–$3,250

create computer-ready photographs from your own camera. Your Photo CD becomes an expandable portfolio of your original photographs that can be used directly by image editing or desktop publishing software.

- Additional *fonts*. While fonts are included with your computer and printer, it will be necessary to purchase additional fonts in order to increase your design capabilities and improve the appearance and originality of your work. Fonts basically come in two formats: PostScript (the classic standard) or TrueType (a newer format, widely becoming popular). As a rule, choose either PostScript or TrueType for all your fonts. Combining the two types can be the cause of inexplicable font conflicts and slow printing.

- *Clip art* is also used by most desktop publishers. Even if you have strong drawing and artistic skills, at times it will be helpful to have computerized art ready for quick placement into a flyer or brochure. With drawing programs such as Illustrator and FreeHand, in many cases you can edit clip art, pulling out certain elements, resizing and reshaping, combining it with other art, coloring, and otherwise changing the art to make it unique and more suited to your clients' specific needs. To supplement computerized clip art, look in your bookstore for books of clip art. With a scanner you can easily convert these graphics to editable form, and you'll find a great variety of art that is not overused in desktop-published documents. (You can also revert to old-fashioned cut-and-paste on occasion—a quick, easy, and inexpensive way to add graphics to a document. Try Dryline adhesive cartridges for no-mess application of repositionable glue.)

Office Equipment and Supplies

Your computer and software are your major business purchases, involving the most thought and expense. Other equipment you will need for start-up includes the following:

- *Office furniture*. Desks, filing cabinets, bookcases, shelves—all are required but need not be expensive. Examine options for using furniture you already have, such as bookcases and tables, and be on the lookout for used-office-furniture sales. "Musts" include a large work surface; chairs and a table or desk for meeting with clients and reviewing their work, if they will be coming to your office; storage space for files and office supplies; and an office chair. A high-quality, supportive, adjustable, ergonomically correct chair is a sound investment in your health and comfort and is not an area where you should scrimp.

- *Telephone.* An ideal setup is a two-line phone with built-in answering capabilities. You will need at least two phone lines—one for business (a business listing is a requirement to advertise in the Yellow Pages) and one for residential use. A third line, for your fax machine, is an agreeable luxury but is definitely not a necessity. Your fax line can be shared with either of your two lines—preferably the residence line, so you don't tie up your business line when receiving or sending faxes. If it's available in your area, I recommend a very inexpensive service that provides an additional telephone number with a distinctive ring without an additional installed line. For many years I used the distinctive ring for my fax number and shared it with my residence line.

  A hold button is an essential feature for your office phones and should be considered for *all* phones if you are frequently out of the office and in other parts of the house during normal business hours. Using the hold button allows you to scoot back to your office and pick up the line there, where you have client files, paper, and pen readily at hand. The hold button can also be used on the (hopefully rare) occasions when you need to quell or escape from children's voices or other household noises that have risen to a level that might be heard by your caller.

  Cordless phones provide flexibility to move about the office while speaking on the phone. This is a wonderful convenience and, if you have young children at home, can be a real lifesaver—you can dash into a quiet room to complete a phone call if household noise erupts within the office. As well, having the portable phone by your side means you can work anywhere you like, including outside or in a quiet room of your home. Computer equipment may cause static in some cordless phones. If you purchase one, try it out in your office while all the equipment is on. If you experience a great deal of static, exchange the phone for a different model. Newer cordless phones with multichannel capabilities may alleviate this problem.

I have experimented with a telephone headset (similar to those worn by operators), but I found the reception less than perfect and the cord somewhat entangling. I know several business owners who swear by them, though, so if you find you are spending lengthy periods on the telephone, or if you experience neck and shoulder pain from cradling the phone against your ear for long periods of time, you should investigate headsets. They are available through office-supply companies as well as specialized telephone stores and catalogs.

- *Answering machine.* Your answering machine should enable callers to leave messages of any length. Having a tape (rather than internal) system for recording outgoing messages is helpful. You can then record two or three different messages—for vacations, days when you are in or out of the office, etc.—and simply switch the tapes as necessary rather than rerecording your messages. Voice-mail service, available in most areas through the telephone company, is a high-quality answering service that you may wish to consider. One advantage to voice mail is that calls coming in while you are on the phone are picked up by voice mail and, thus, the caller doesn't get a busy signal. You might wish to consider call-waiting, a service that interrupts with a clicking noise when another call is coming in while you are speaking on the phone. I don't recommend it—I find it intrusive, and many callers dislike being interrupted and put on hold while you answer another call. One way to keep your business phone line open is to make outgoing calls on your residence line. (This may also be a cost-saving strategy if, as is typical in parts of the country, you are assessed per-call charges on a business line but have unlimited local usage on a residence line.)

- *Fax machine.* A fax machine is a necessity for a desktop publishing business—the back-and-forth exchange of text, drafts, proofs, and graphic elements is a part of every business day. Features to look for on a fax machine include a fine-resolution mode, useful for sending small-size text or complex graphics for improved readability on the receiving end; a document-stacker, so that you can stick a number of sheets to be faxed into the send area, push a button, and walk away, rather than having to feed each sheet individually; a paper cutter for incoming faxes; the ability to store frequently used fax numbers for one-touch faxing; and delayed-sending and group-faxing features, for cost savings and convenience.

It's possible to use an inexpensive internal *fax/modem* within your computer, but it's more practical to purchase a separate fax machine. With just a fax/modem, you must leave your computer on at all times to allow you to receive faxes, and everything that is faxed out must be generated on the computer (either keyboarded or scanned in).

■ *Photocopier.* While not a necessity, you will certainly find owning a copy machine a convenience. Look for reduction and enlargement features and the ability to copy on different weights of stock. A useful feature not found on many small-office photocopiers is a document feeder, which eliminates the need for you to copy each sheet in a stack of papers individually. Check into both leasing and purchasing a copier. Leasing, while more costly in a direct-dollar comparison, means less capital outlay on your part and also offers the ability to trade in (trading up *or* down, depending on your experience with use of the machine) when the lease period is up. Many small businesses don't start out with a copy machine but, when they finally get one, wonder how they did without it for so long! This may be another item to place near the top of your acquisitions list if it's not affordable on start-up.

■ *Office supplies.* Locate at least two good sources for office supplies, preferably one mail order and one local retailer. Mail order is extremely practical because you can order at your convenience—usually by toll-free phone or fax—and have supplies delivered right to your door, typically within one to three days. As well, prices are usually extremely competitive. For those last-minute emergencies or to actually compare products, a local supplier is your best choice. Superstore retailers such as Staples, Office Max, and Office Depot, found in different parts of the country, are fast becoming the standard for office supplies. They have a large selection and low prices and may offer phone-in ordering with next-day delivery as well as local shopping convenience. You might find it beneficial to patronize a small, local office supply store and develop a relationship with the owner(s). If their business is thriving with all the superstore competition, it's likely due to an exceptional level of service—something you might like to take advantage of.

Basic supplies to have on hand include paper (inexpensive copy paper for drafts and photocopies, higher-quality laser paper for final output), stapler/staples/staple remover, paper clips, tape, scissors, X-acto knife, glue stick, ruler, blank diskettes, pens and markers (including red for proofreading), correcting fluid, scratch pads, fax paper, blank labels, envelopes (plain white #10 plus 9x12 for sending pages flat), file folders, a postal scale and postage in a variety of denominations (first class, second ounce, postcard, Priority and Express mail), a hand-held or printing calculator, and a good-sized wastebasket.

With the ready availability of office supplies on short notice, there is no need to lay in large quantities of supplies. It makes sense to buy paper by the carton (ten reams) and to purchase pens by the box rather than individually; but with other items, single or small quantities will be sufficient. Flipping through the pages of an office supply catalog will help you compile a "wish list" of products you'd like to have for your office but don't necessarily need from day one. These include three-hole punches, paper cutters, disk storage boxes, electric staplers and pencil sharpeners, and so on.

■ *Business cards, stationery, and envelopes.* Here is your first desktop design project! A supply of these items should be on hand before you open for business, for use in dealing with vendors and suppliers, networking, contacting professional organizations, sending press releases and other media communications, and being prepared from day one to present yourself as a professional, established business. Since these items say a good deal about you and your business, they need to be attractive and of high quality and make an excellent visual impression. There is no excuse for a desktop publishing professional to have ordinary, plain-Jane business cards of the type available from any print shop or business-supply catalog. This is an opportunity for you to demonstrate your DTP skills for your own benefit. Once you have decided on your business name, you can begin to experiment with design ideas that communicate your desired image. After you have come up with a few preliminary designs, share them with friends and

START-UP ESTIMATES

OFFICE EQUIPMENT AND SUPPLIES

ITEM	PRICE RANGE
Office furniture: desk, chairs, file cabinets	$400–$2,500
Telephone/answering machine	$80–$300
Telephone service (monthly cost $40–$75)	$480–$900
Fax machine	$250–$400
Copy machine	$1,000–$2,500
Office supplies	$150–$350
Business cards, stationery, envelopes	$75–$200
TOTAL: Office Equipment and Supplies	$2,435–$7,150

ADDITIONAL START-UP EXPENSES

ITEM	PRICE RANGE
Business checking account and checks	$25–$75
Business insurance	$25–$400
Business sign	$50–$250
Advertising (monthly $150–$500)	$1,800–$6,000
TOTAL: Additional Start-up Expenses	$1,900–$6,725

family members to get their reactions. Then refine your ideas till you are satisfied. Consider printing in color or on unusual paper to make your materials stand out. Once you have established a logo and/or a professional image for your company, you should be prepared to live with it for a long while, so take the time to come up with something that is attractive and represents your business well. This is another excellent opportunity for relationship-building with a local printer—bring in your design and get his or her opinion about paper choices and colors. Printers, who see both amateur and professional DTP work on a daily basis, will recognize the quality and originality of your work, and this will make a positive impression on them—quite possibly leading to future referrals and a mutually supportive business relationship.

Chapter 5 provides additional tips on using business cards as sales tools.

In addition to a quantity of stationery and envelopes, consider ordering your letterhead printed on inexpensive white paper in black ink, to use for memos and invoices.

Business cards are usually ordered in quantities of 500 or 1,000. For start-up, 500 will be sufficient. There's a chance that you will change or acquire information, such as a new fax number or e-mail address, so it's best to be conservative for your first printing so that you don't end up with hundreds of unusable business cards.

Other Preopening Needs

In addition to the equipment and supplies described above, a variety of other planning and preopening activities need to be addressed.

It's essential to keep accurate and detailed *records* of your business expenses (and income, once you start earning it!). All legitimate business expenses are offset against your income, and the resulting total becomes your taxable income. For tax purposes, your goal will be to make your net income, and thus your tax liability, as low as possible. Thus, recording and accounting for all your business expenses is in your own best interest. In addition to tracking all costs with your bookkeeping system (either manual or computerized), you should obtain and file receipts for every one of your expenditures. (Refer to chapter 6 for more information on record keeping.)

You will need a *business checking account;* ideally, look for a bank that offers convenient services such as ATM or night deposits, drive-up tellers, banking by mail, and low- or no-cost accounts. "DBA" (doing-business-as) accounts, offered by some banks, are the equivalent of personal checking accounts in your business name and are usually the most economical. Investigate various sources for check printing. Often mail-order checks are less expensive than those supplied by banks. If you plan to use financial-management software (such as Quicken) that enables you to write checks on the computer, you can order the appropriate checks through most check printers, not just through the software company.

Business insurance—both property and liability coverage—should be in place before you begin conducting business. In many cases, an inexpensive rider to your homeowner's insurance will cover your business equipment in the event of theft, fire, or other damage. Liability insurance is intended to protect your personal assets should you be sued for damages by a client. Although the likelihood of this happening is slim, it's wise to have protection in place so you are well prepared for any eventuality. You may also wish to consider disability insurance to provide some level of income in the event you become unable to work. My experience has been that disability insurance requires a high premium for a relatively low income replacement, so I have elected not to purchase it. Your own decision might be different, particularly if you are your family's sole support.

If you are planning to have a *business sign*—and you can do so in accordance with zoning requirements—give some thought to signage that will identify your business yet not detract from the residential appearance of your home. Your goal should be to make it easy for clients to identify your business. If your residence is an apartment or condo, a business sign may be particularly important to assist clients in finding you. Whether or not you have a sign, prepare a set of clear directions to your location from various well-known points. This will require that you actually drive the route, measuring distances and rechecking landmarks. It's extremely disconcerting for a client to be given rambling directions or, even worse, to be directed according to landmarks that no longer exist. I have never used a business sign, preferring to identify my location by my house number, displayed prominently on both my mailbox and the front of my home. I also use the color of my home and its location at the end of a cul-de-sac as easy identifiers.

Your *advertising* and *marketing* efforts and their related costs are another significant expense to include in your initial planning. Although marketing and advertising are essential at any stage, in the start-up phase they are crucial to the success of the business. So it's critical that you devise a consistent, organized, and ongoing marketing and advertising effort that will last throughout your first year. There are numerous no- and low-cost strategies you can use to increase your prospective clients' awareness of your business, so your efforts in this area are not entirely dependent on your budget. (See chapter 5 for more information.) To develop these costs during your planning stage, count on purchasing twelve months' worth of Yellow Pages advertising and spending perhaps an equal amount for other forms of advertising, direct mail, and various sales and marketing materials. (Yellow Pages advertising is billed at a monthly rate and is included in your local phone bill, even though the directory is published once a year.)

The cost estimates given here include both start-up and ongoing costs for your first year in business. It's quite possible—and very common—for businesses to start without a full complement of all desired equipment. For instance, I purchased my presentation software immediately *after* I had assured a prospective client that I could prepare slides for the following week! Depending on your finances, you may be able to acquire all the equipment, supplies, and services you need before actually launching your business. More likely, however, you will make the most essential purchases to start with and then develop a prioritized list for acquisition as soon as you have an immediate need or can afford it.

DETERMINING YOUR RATE STRUCTURE

Establishing rates can be one of the most daunting tasks in a service business. To arrive at an appropriate hourly rate, begin by reviewing the competitive data you collected earlier. What are your competitors' rates? What do those rates include? This information provides you with a general range of acceptable desktop publishing rates in your area. Desktop publishing prices for all areas of the country are detailed in Robert Brenner's book, *Pricing Guide for Desktop Publishing Services* (see the Appendix for complete information). This is another way to check your competitiveness with the range in your locality.

Now it's time to determine what you need to charge in order to cover your ongoing expenses; allow for continual purchase and upgrading of equipment, software, etc.; pay taxes; pay yourself a salary; and, it is hoped, make a profit! It is normal and expected for start-up expenses to be higher than annual ongoing expenses (although you may be able to deduct the entire cost of your start-up equipment on the current year's tax return—check IRS guidelines for capital equipment purchases). Naturally, you will not need to purchase a new computer, printer, copier, scanner, complete software packages, and office furniture every year. You will, however, need to allocate funds for these purchases so that when the time comes that you need new equipment, you can afford to buy it. With this goal in mind, you should include in your financial plan a set-aside for *capital acquisitions*.

There are other expenses that will occur on an annual basis that should be included in your analysis but that we have not addressed in the previous section on start-up costs. These include:

- *Salary*. Although you may initially be willing to take whatever's left over after meeting all your expenses, it is wise to include a projected salary for yourself in your planning. It's easy to assume your business is profitable when you are earning more than you are spending, but unless you are also paying yourself a reasonable salary, your profitability figures will not be realistic.

- *Self-employment tax; federal and state income taxes.* These figures will vary depending upon your income (total income, if you file a joint return with your spouse) and your state regulations. Since you are now self-employed, taxes are no longer taken out of a paycheck. Instead, they are calculated on your annual tax returns and paid at the time you file your return. (If your tax return indicates a large payment of taxes at tax filing time, you will be required to make quarterly tax payments in subsequent years.) Figure on 15 percent for self-employment tax and another 25 to 40 percent for federal, state, and local income taxes (assessed in some areas), depending on your income. If you file jointly with your spouse, your business income is not considered separately but is added to his or her total income—so you can count on paying your top tax rate on any income from your business. During your first year or two of business, when expenses are high and income is lowest, your tax liability will probably be quite small. Soon, though, you will start to make money—and along with that delightful benefit, you will incur tax liabilities. Assuming that your business is a sole proprietorship, your tax liability will be incurred on your *net profit*—the amount left over after calculating all expenses except salary. Since you are the business owner and not technically an employee, any salary you pay yourself is not a deductible expense; instead, it is added to other profit to establish your taxable income.

■ *Professional services.* You may wish to consult an attorney or an accountant at start-up or for assistance during the course of the year. Accountants, in particular, can be very helpful in working through the maze of financial, tax, and reporting requirements that are involved in business ownership—and they may more than pay for their services by saving you money on your tax return. Professional services relating to your business are legitimate and deductible expenses.

■ *Memberships, dues, subscriptions, meetings, conferences, education.* Joining organizations in your community is an excellent way to make contacts that will help your business. Costs for joining these organizations and attending regular meetings are tax-deductible expenses. As well, if you take training courses or attend conferences to further your skills, you may deduct the cost of these activities. Subscriptions to business-related periodicals are also a legitimate business expense.

■ *Business use of your home.* Home-based businesses do not have the expense of a monthly rent check, but figuring in a percentage of your utilities and other household expenses will give a more realistic picture of your business costs—and many of these items will be tax-deductible business expenses. The IRS offers specific guidelines for business use of your home, and you can use their publications to determine your own figures. Generally, a percentage of your household expenses—such as utilities (electricity, gas, oil), home maintenance, repairs, cleaning, snow plowing, lawn mowing, trash removal, security system, and other expenses that are not paid for directly by the business, as well as home depreciation—is figured, based on the square footage percentage of your home used by your business.

- *Automobile expenses.* Business use of your car is a legitimate and tax-deductible expense. There are two ways to calculate this expense: 1) take a standard mileage deduction (per IRS guidelines) for each business mile traveled during the year; 2) figure the percentage represented by business use of your vehicle, then apply that percentage to all automobile costs during the year (gas, repairs, maintenance, lease payments, etc.). It is recommended that during your first few years in business, you track your actual mileage; then, if it is consistent from year to year, you may utilize that percentage for future years. Keep a notebook and pen in your car and jot down starting and ending mileage each time you make a business-related trip. Once a month, enter the mileage totals into your financial records.

- *Health insurance.* As you will find, health insurance for self-employed individuals is expensive and not always easy to obtain. If you are married, your best bet will probably be to obtain insurance through your spouse's employer. Check with other self-employed people you know to get information on health insurance options. Membership in an organization such as the Chamber of Commerce or another professional group sometimes provides opportunities to purchase health insurance at group rates.

- *Retirement plan.* It's essential to include some long-range planning in your expense estimates. If you establish a self-employed retirement account (SEP), the IRS allows you to deposit up to 15 percent of your net earnings (up to $30,000 annually) and deduct this amount from your tax liability.

- *Vendor/subcontractor expenses.* For the purposes of this exercise, let's assume that this cost will be a "break-even" expense—amounts billed to clients will cover your costs for vendors and subcontractors, resulting in neither income nor expense to your business.

- *Equipment maintenance.* If your equipment is new, it will have a warranty for a specific time period—usually a minimum of ninety days. Try to negotiate an extended warranty when making your purchase. This service can be provided at low or no cost to the retailer but is very valuable to you. Depending on costs in your area, it is usually a good idea to have service contracts on your major equipment—computer, printer(s), copier—since the costs and time loss from malfunctions of this equipment can have a serious impact on your business.

- *Miscellaneous office expenses.* These include overnight delivery, postage, various supplies, and other items not accounted for in the previous line items.

Complete the blank Expense Summary provided, using your own cost estimates, to get a total picture of your cost of doing business on an annual basis. (A filled-in example, with hypothetical numbers, is given for illustration purposes—these numbers may not be applicable to your own unique circumstances.)

How Much Can You Expect to Earn?

The salary figure given in the expense summary example is hypothetical, as are all the numbers, but naturally you want to know how much you can reasonably expect to earn as a desktop publisher. As reported in Robert Brenner's *Pricing Guide for Desktop Publishing Services*, sole-proprietor DTP businesses earned annual gross incomes ranging from $1,000 to $875,000, while independent owner-operator businesses reported incomes from $1,000 to $95,000. (Keep in mind that these are gross incomes and do not reflect actual profit after expenses.) The profitability of your own business will be affected by many factors, including the number of hours you work, average rates in your area, how effectively you control expenses, how rapidly you are able to build your business, and so on. It is reasonable to expect, however, that once your business is established, you will be able to earn as much as or more than desktop publishing professionals working full-time for another company in your area. Many of us in the business expect to earn *considerably* more—after all, we work hard and long and assume substantial risks. Don't open a desktop publishing business expecting to get rich, but do expect to earn a comfortable living.

How Much Do You Need to Charge?

Continuing with the pricing exercise, let's consider the number of hours you are able to work—and the number you are able to bill. These two numbers are not the same! In any business, nonbillable tasks will take up a certain amount of your time. Typical nonbillable activities include invoicing,

EXPENSE SUMMARY

ESTIMATED COSTS

Capital equipment (new/replacement equipment fund) $ _____

Software (new/upgrades, fonts, clip art, etc.)   _____

Telephone line(s)   _____

Office supplies   _____

Marketing materials/printing   _____

Business insurance   _____

Yellow Pages   _____

Advertising (other than Yellow Pages)   _____

Salary   _____

Self-employment tax; federal and state income taxes   _____

Professional services   _____

Memberships, dues, subscriptions   _____

Business use of home   _____

Automobile expenses   _____

Maintenance agreements   _____

Miscellaneous   _____

TOTAL ESTIMATED ANNUAL EXPENSES $ _____

EXPENSE SUMMARY

ESTIMATED COSTS

Capital equipment (new/replacement equipment fund)	$ 1,200
Software (new/upgrades, fonts, clip art, etc.)	400
Telephone line(s)	700
Office supplies	1,400
Marketing materials/printing	400
Business insurance	300
Yellow Pages	1,500
Advertising and marketing (other than Yellow Pages)	2,400
Salary	30,000
Self-employment tax; federal and state income taxes	13,500
Professional services	600
Memberships, dues, subscriptions	500
Business use of home	2,000
Automobile expenses	1,200
Maintenance agreements	300
Miscellaneous	2,000
TOTAL ESTIMATED ANNUAL EXPENSES	**$ 57,200**

bookkeeping, marketing, answering the phone, emptying trash, dusting and vacuuming your office, running errands, ordering supplies, clearing up printer or copier jams, troubleshooting software bugs, and learning a new program. A good rule to follow when estimating billable/nonbillable time is the 75/25 rule—75 percent of your time will be spent on billable work, while 25 percent will go toward nonbillable tasks.

Keeping this in mind, figure the total number of hours you are able to work yearly. A 45-hour work week equates to 33.75 billable hours. Allow yourself four weeks for vacations, holidays, sick time, conferences, etc. Therefore, multiplying 33.75 (hours weekly) times 48 (available weeks) gives you a total of 1,620 billable hours annually.

If you would prefer to work fewer hours, recalculate the equation using a 35-hour work week—or 26.25 billable hours: 26.25 x 48 = 1,260 billable hours annually.

Knowing your total number of available billable hours is important because you will use it to determine the *minimum amount* you need to charge to cover your expenses and stay in business.

For the purposes of this exercise, let's take the average of the two examples—assume a 40-hour work week, resulting in 30 billable hours for a total of 1,440 billable hours annually. Using the estimated expenses on the sample worksheet, you can see that the minimum hourly rate necessary is $39.72.

Keep this number in mind as you establish rates for all the services you provide. For instance, $40 per hour may not be an acceptable rate for word processing/data entry in your area, so you might plan to price this service at $20 per hour—or half of the minimum hourly rate established in our example. If you envision spending one-quarter of your time doing word processing, you will have to charge $47 per hour for desktop publishing in order to average your desired hourly rate of $40.

You've probably noticed that this formula assumes that you will be able to bill the full 75 percent of available hours—in other words, you will have enough work to keep you busy for twenty-five or thirty-five billable hours a week. This is a very optimistic assumption for your first year or two in business, when your business name and client base are not yet well established. It is more likely that during this start-up phase, increased time will be spent on marketing activities to generate additional work. Consequently, additional advertising and printing costs will probably accrue, while office supplies may decrease—as will your salary, in all likeli-hood. Also, no provision is made here for business profit (above and beyond your salary) or SEP retirement contributions. It would be a good idea to repeat this exercise annually, to determine if your rates are suffi-cient to cover your expenses given your actual experience in the business whether your own schesule follows the 75/25 rule and to factor in long-range retirement plans once your business is underway.

Speaking of annual review, many service businesses apply an auto-matic annual rate increase. Making such an increase part of your busi-ness policy is one way to eliminate the sometimes-agonizing decision: Should I or shouldn't I raise my rates? If one year you decide not to increase your rates, because of a difficult economy or other factors, this is an easy and positive message to pass along to your clients.

Go through this exercise, using your own numbers, to determine your minimum. Then compare it to average rates in your area. Is it close? If it's considerably higher or lower than the average, review your figures to see if you've made a miscalculation or forgotten to include an item.

Now, armed with this information—averages for your area, your own minimum requirements—you are ready to set your hourly rates.

It's likely you will establish more than one hourly rate, depending on the specific services you plan to provide. Typically, word processing and less-complex office support tasks command lower hourly figures, while desktop publishing is more highly priced. Graphic design can easily com-mand a still higher rate.

Pricing Rationale

While you may be tempted to price your services just below the lowest in your area, in hopes of capturing price-conscious clients, this is probably not the best way to begin your business. Unless you are a very large oper-ation and can produce a high volume of work, you cannot hope to com-pete on price unless you are willing to either work more hours or earn less money than your competitors—or both! In addition, setting your prices too low means that you will have to raise them before long, just to stay in business. And, although with this tactic you will undoubtedly attract bargain hunters, an equally large number of clients will stay away from bargain-basement desktop publishers due to concerns about qual-ity, longevity, and professionalism.

It's typical for small, new businesses—particularly if they are home-based—to make the mistake of charging too little at the outset. Although it's true that your out-of-pocket expenses will be lower if you are home-based, and you may be willing to work long hours for little reward when you are starting out, remember that you're in business for the long run. Your success depends on your ability to make a profit, and you deserve to be fairly compensated for your time, investment in equipment, and expertise in your field. Also, keep in mind that your expense estimates are just that—estimates. You'll be better off erring on the high side in establishing your rates, in order to cover unexpected, unanticipated, or incorrectly estimated expenses.

The price you set on your services plays a vital role in their perceived value. Think about it. Why do some people buy a Mercedes when they could drive a Toyota? Why do they stay at the Ritz instead of the Holiday Inn? In each instance, they are purchasing the same commodity: a means of transportation; overnight accommodations. Yet they are purchasing—or *believe* they are purchasing—a superior experience when they spend more money for the Mercedes or the Ritz. So Mercedes-Benz and the Ritz-Carlton are invested in ensuring that they provide that higher-quality experience, while Toyota and Holiday Inn are committed to providing value for the dollar. The experience is similar with desktop publishing. Some clients will always want what they perceive as the "best"—usually the most expensive—service. Others will go for the "best value"—the lowest price, or the most for their money. The largest percentage of clients will choose a service somewhere in the middle, based on price *and* what they perceive as additional benefits or services. Your job, then, is to convince that middle-ground client that *you* provide the benefits and services he or she is looking for, while charging a reasonable price—neither too high nor too low. A small, home-based business is in an excellent position to compete on quality and service. (You can read more about this in chapter 5.)

In desktop publishing, two rate structures are typical: billing by the hour or by the project. Occasionally, you might be asked to provide a per-page rate. In any of these instances, you need to know your hourly rate so that you can base your estimates on the time it will take to do the work. (There's more about project estimates and billing in chapters 6 and 7.)

WRITING A BUSINESS PLAN

The difference between running your business *with* a business plan and *without* one can be compared to driving a car *with* and *without* a firm destination in mind. Imagine you're out for a Sunday ride. You decide you'd like to drive to the coast to admire the sun on the water. Halfway there you are distracted by a farmers' market and stop to do some shopping. Then, getting back in your car, you remember that an old friend lives in the neighborhood, so you stop by and spend an hour or so chatting and drinking lemonade. Returning to your vehicle, you realize it's too late to drive all the way to the coast, so instead you head for a nearby lake, where you take a short hike and enjoy the beauty of the outdoors. Although you didn't achieve your initial goal—driving to the coast—you certainly had an enjoyable day, with a good variety of activities.

The next day you get in your car again to head to work. You are determined to try a new route to avoid traffic, which has been very heavy lately on the roads you usually travel. You encounter an unexpected road block that forces you to detour a bit out of your way, but soon you are able to resume your planned route. You spot a side road that looks like it might be a promising alternative, but you decide to wait to try it until you can check a map to see where it eventually leads. You arrive at work with a feeling of satisfaction and accomplishment, having traveled your planned route and learned a new way to work.

In a similar manner, you can enjoy and profit from your business with or without a business plan. You may have certain vague or unspoken goals in mind and work to accomplish them, but since they are not specifically stated or written objectives, you feel free to change your plans when you spot something that looks like it might be profitable or enjoyable. You enjoy flexibility, but you also may never achieve your initial goal—or even set one.

Using a business plan, you give thought to where you would like to end up in a year, two years, five years, and how you're going to get there—your road map. This leads to specific goals and plans—and the ability to swerve around road blocks and unexpected detours and focus again as soon as possible on achieving your goal. You retain the ability to change directions, but before doing so you evaluate the new direction and possibly revise your business plan.

In addition to being important to overall goal achievement, a business plan is essential if you plan to approach a bank for financing for your business. As well, family members and friends who may be lending money for your venture will be impressed by your clear plans—and the means by which you envision achieving them. Writing a business plan demonstrates that you have thought carefully about your proposed new venture, that you have done research and given due consideration to all aspects of your business, not just to the desktop publishing functions.

A general outline of a business plan is presented below, with information on how to prepare each section. You'll find that the planning you've done already, discussed earlier in this chapter, will provide you with most of the essential information you'll need.

If you are using a business plan to approach a bank, you will need to prepare a very thorough document that complies with the expected business-plan format. There are numerous good, detailed books on this subject, available at bookstores and libraries. In addition, there is now available computer software that helps you write a business plan. It presents the major topic areas and guidelines and guides you as you fill in the information. If this possibility interests you, check online resources or the indexes of computer and business magazines to find recent reviews of business-plan software.

Parts of a Business Plan

Executive Summary: This is a summary of your entire plan, a general description of your business, and a description of your qualifications to run it. The Executive Summary typically is written last, after you have completed all the detail required for the other sections of the plan. This section is, however, read first and should be a strong sales pitch for you and your business—factual yet optimistic and reflective of your unique attributes.

Business Description: Here you provide a detailed description of your services. Describe your anticipated clients and explain how they are going to find out about and utilize your services. Your type of business organization (most commonly sole proprietorship) should be mentioned, along with financial information—specifically, your anticipated revenues. For this section, use the information you have already developed regarding your market niche as well as general income estimates based on an analysis of your expenses and rates.

Market Analysis: The information you have gathered about your competitors is the basis for this section of the business plan. After describing the competing businesses in your area, indicate how you will fill a particular need or market niche; in other words, give some indication of why there is a need for an additional desktop publishing service in your area. Significant industry trends, such as the proliferation of personal computers in both homes and offices or the recent emergence of desktop color printers, should also be addressed, along with your planned responses to these trends. For example, you can state that you plan to work collaboratively with your clients to give a professional polish to documents they draft on their computers; or you might indicate that you will provide color printing services to small businesses that are not yet equipped with this technology.

Management and Operational Plan: Here is where you describe the nuts-and-bolts operation of your business. If you are the only employee, give pertinent information on your background and expertise in as many aspects of the business as possible (for instance, desktop publishing, graphic design, business operations, office management, marketing and sales). Describe how you plan to use vendors and subcontractors to round out your service offerings, and give their specific names and areas of expertise if you have already established preliminary relationships with them. Discuss your equipment and how you will utilize it.

Marketing Strategy: How do you plan to attract clients? (Review chapter 5 for pertinent information on this topic.) Describe all your advertising, promotional, and marketing plans. Again, mention any market niche you are targeting and how you plan to appeal to clients in this market.

Financial Plan: An Expense Worksheet, a Balance Sheet, and a Profit-and-Loss Statement should be prepared utilizing information from your estimates of start-up and ongoing expenses and estimated income:

- The *Expense Worksheet* can be based on the Expense Summary you developed when establishing your rate structure. It should be summarized monthly, however, instead of annually, and can include a more detailed itemized listing.

- The *Balance Sheet* is a detailed listing of all your assets and your liabilities (which total each other out, equaling zero).

- The *Profit-and-Loss Statement* is a yearly (or possibly monthly) summary of actual income and expenditures. It does not include your salary; instead, any income exceeding expenses is referred to as "Profit."

In this section of the business plan, indicate how you will acquire financing for your start-up (savings, anticipated bank loan, investments by family members, credit cards, and so on) and how you will pay it back, if necessary. Be sure to include in your income estimates any projected rate increases and the continual enlargement of your client base.

Appendix: Your resume should be included as an attachment to the business plan. Also include your letterhead and business card showing your logo, if you have developed one; letters of reference from past employers and potential clients; and any other material that supports the assertions you have made in the business plan, such as relevant newspaper articles about you or your industry, market research studies, and the like.

Using Your Business Plan

Once you have completed your business plan, share it with interested friends and relatives and, if applicable, use it to apply for bank financing. Be sure to keep a copy to review every six months to a year, to remind you of your original destination and the "road map" you planned to use. If you find yourself off track, you may wish either to revise your business plan to encompass new goals, or to rededicate yourself to the task of completing your original plan. Setting this information down on paper ensures it will not be forgotten.

If you plan to apply for a bank loan, be prepared with your business plan before you visit the bank. Demonstrating that you have done your homework and given serious consideration to all aspects of your business will impress lenders—and your request for funds will not be seriously considered without a business plan. If you are applying for a loan, don't make the mistake of many small businesses and ask for too little money. True, you don't want to be burdened with large repayments, but having the essential cash to start your business the right way will go a long way toward ensuring a successful start-up, with the equipment and security you need.

The current economic climate and the prevalence (or lack of) home-based businesses in your area will greatly affect your bank's decision to grant a loan. If you are unsuccessful at getting bank financing, examine other options. It's likely your most pressing need will be for capital equipment. You will also need to have available funds for at least six months of operating expenses, as well as your necessary living expenses. Many small businesses are funded by loans from friends and family members. These are people who know you and are likely to believe you will be successful—even if you weren't able to convince a bank. If you do borrow from friends and family, structure a written interest and repayment agreement to be sure the terms of the loan are clearly understood. Trusting to oral agreements leaves open the possibility for misunderstandings and hard feelings that can adversely affect your relationships.

While you are planning for your business, you may be able to amass some seed money by cutting back on your expenses and adhering to a rigorous savings program. Being able to start up without borrowing money will give you fewer worries, although your financial cushion may be less comfortable. You also may be able to utilize a personal line of credit from a home equity loan or credit cards. Remember, you are really making an investment in yourself and your dream—and no one will ever be more committed than you to making your dream a reality.

STARTING YOUR BUSINESS PART-TIME OR WITH LIMITED RESOURCES

One of the biggest advantages to a home-based, service-oriented business is the complete flexibility it affords you, the business owner. It is entirely feasible to start a home-based DTP business on a part-time basis, perhaps while holding down another full-time job—you'll be making valuable connections with people who can be of great help as your new enterprise gets off the ground. What is more, if your funds are severely limited and you cannot afford to invest much beyond the cost of a basic computer, limited DTP software, and a printer, you can still make a start and expand your investment as your funds allow. The information provided in this book will apply in each of these circumstances, although you will naturally have to scale back income projections (as well as expenses) and may not be able to spend as much time as recommended in some of the various activities. Plan carefully and concentrate on those activities that require less investment of time or money—whichever commodity is scarcer. But don't give up your dream.

Once you've completed the extensive planning necessary for a successful start-up, you're nearly ready to open your doors to your first client! Use the following planning summaries and check off items as you complete them.

PLANNING CHECKLIST:
GENERAL AND REGULATORY INFORMATION

ITEM	SCHEDULED DATE	COMPLETED ✔	NOTES
Review books/library			
Review books/bookstores			
Review magazines and newsletters			
Look into professional and networking organizations			
Competition survey: Yellow Pages Local publications Networking groups			
Conduct telephone survey: competitors			
Determine service mix			
Contact vendors: 1. 2. 3. 4. 5.			
Call Town Hall re: business registration			
Check on zoning requirements			
Check on home-based restrictions			
Call state re: sales taxes			
Check with lawyer/accountant re: business structure			

PLANNING CHECKLIST: EQUIPMENT AND SUPPLIES

ITEM	SCHEDULED DATE	COMPLETED ✔	NOTES
Computer-system research			
Computer-system purchase			
Scanner research/purchase			
Printer research/purchase			
Color printer research/purchase			

Major software research
   1.
   2.
   3.			

Major software purchase
   1.
   2.
   3.			

Additional software research
   1.
   2.
   3.			

Additional software purchase
   1.
   2.
   3.			

Office furniture research			
Office furniture purchase			
Research/purchase telephone			
Research/purchase fax			
Research copy machines			

Office supplies: locate vendors
   1.
   2.			

PLANNING CHECKLIST: ADDITIONAL REQUIREMENTS

ITEM	SCHEDULED DATE	COMPLETED ✔	NOTES
Open business checking account			
Set up business financial records			

Research/purchase business insurance:
    Homeowner rider
    Liability
    Disability			

Design business cards & stationery			
Print business cards & stationery			
Investigate signage requirements			
Order business sign			
Compile info for business plan			
Write business plan			
Investigate personal financial resources (credit cards, home equity loan)			
Meet with banker			
Meet with friends/family members re: financing			
Establish business name			
Set up rate structure			
Set up office			
Initiate marketing campaign Prepare and send press release			
OPEN FOR BUSINESS!			

CHAPTER FOUR

SETTING UP YOUR OFFICE

A place for everything, and everything in its place.

— SAMUEL SMILES

ith the goal of establishing a home-based business, no doubt you have in mind a certain part of your home to use for office space. This chapter will address factors to consider in setting up and arranging your office and other aspects of home-business organization.

SELECTING YOUR OFFICE SPACE

First, let's consider the ideal home office. It's large enough to accommodate your work area, related equipment, and client meeting space. It has ample storage behind closed doors—cabinets or a closet into which you can put the "stuff" that naturally accumulates in a paper-intensive business like desktop publishing. It has lots of light, both natural and artificial. There are numerous electrical outlets, including several with dedicated access so you can run energy-intensive equipment without affecting the energy supply to other outlets on the same wire. The temperature is easily controlled with doors and windows, fans, and/or air conditioning. There is a door leading directly outside, so clients don't have to walk through any other part of your home to get to the office. It provides easy access to the rest of your residence but is not a pathway from one part of the house to another. A lavatory—not the main family bathroom—is situated nearby. The office is attractively decorated and furnished with a full array of office essentials.

Now, let's get real! If your home office has all the features and amenities described above, consider yourself very fortunate. It's more likely that you'll be faced with some positive and some not-so-positive features in your office. Concentrate on those that are most important, and then try to devise ways to work around your limits. You can always add to your list of goals a new home or a dedicated office addition!

My first office was half of my infant daughter's bedroom—less than a perfect setup, but I managed for my first year in business. We then moved to a new home that had a dedicated office that was nearly ideal. It had direct access from the outdoors, closet and shelf space, and nice decor. Its major drawbacks were its small size and the fact that it was the main pathway into the rest of the home. For twelve years I spent more time in that office than any other room in the house, so I got to know its limitations and advantages very well. Over the years we added dedicated outlets, an air conditioner, additional desk space, and ingenious storage solutions. We even redecorated. But we were unable to solve the "walk-through" problem, and the office always felt crowded.

I came to appreciate the advantages of my home office most fully while it was being remodeled. During the several weeks it took to apply new paint and wallpaper and install new carpeting, I temporarily relocated my office in a sun porch off my family room. I greatly enjoyed the large space and ample sunlight there—but I very much disliked having to greet clients at the front door and lead them past living and dining room, through the kitchen and family room, and out to the office. My housekeeping time nearly doubled as I struggled to keep our most lived-in rooms spotless for client walk-throughs. I also missed the ample storage space and a location at the front of the home that afforded me instant notification of anyone driving down the street or approaching the house.

Having recently completed a move to my third home office, I am fortunate to have learned from my past experiences and was able to design the office to meet my needs very closely. Still, I lack hidden storage space and therefore continuously have to be aware of keeping my files, papers, etc., in order—a task that does not come naturally!

There are numerous ways to work around the limitations of your own office space. Let's take a look at some specific areas of importance.

Ideally, try to avoid having your clients walk through other parts of your home to get to your office. If that's unavoidable, try to arrange client entrances through a rather unused part of your home (for example, through the front door and into your office/dining room), and have family members use a different door for most entrances. Having to keep only a small part of your home continually clean and in order is a simple matter compared to having to keep your entire home ready for visitors at all times. Also, it's wise to minimize the impact of client visits on other family members. Keeping your office as isolated as possible makes good sense—and it's helpful, also, if you can work late at night or early in the morning without disturbing family members with light or noise.

If you can't avoid using an out-of-the-way room as your office, think about using a more accessible area for client meetings. You may feel uncomfortable, for instance, leading a client to a bedroom or basement where your office is situated. Instead, set up an area in your living room, dining room, or even a corner of your front entry where you can keep completed client files, intake forms, sample books, and other client-meeting materials, and conduct all client meetings in this area. Keep in mind that a client may wish you to make a quick revision to a document he or she is picking up, and with this setup you will need to excuse yourself and return to your office to make the revision. While this may not be a problem, particularly with a well-known client, consider whether you will feel comfortable leaving clients alone in a part of your home while you are not immediately accessible.

Perhaps your home doesn't have a whole room that you can designate as office. It's perfectly acceptable (including to the IRS) to use part of a room for business purposes, keeping the other part for family use. This type of set-up does make it harder to isolate your work and equipment from the rest of the family, but don't give up your dream of business ownership just because your home doesn't have a spare room. Give extra thought to setting up your office to minimize clutter and keep your office space as distinct as possible.

If your home-office situation is less than desirable, offer to meet clients at their offices. There is no need to explain or apologize for your situation; your clients will probably be delighted to have you offer to travel to their location for meetings. I have had clients who never knew that my business was home-based—I met with them in their offices initially, and then used courier or overnight delivery services when I could not get away to deliver their work. It was not that I tried to hide the fact that I worked at home; it just was immaterial and never came up in our conversations.

Access to a bathroom is something else you should consider. While you may prefer not to offer clients this amenity, it's inevitable that some clients will ask. It's very difficult to refuse access to a bathroom when they certainly know you have one! Therefore, it's incumbent upon you to keep the nearest bathroom clean and free from family clutter. Keep this factor in mind if and when you do any remodeling of your home to accommodate your office.

You should also consider the image that first meets clients' eyes as they approach your business. In a private home, it will be your responsibility to see that outside areas are meticulously maintained and free from hazards. If you live in an apartment or condominium, you must monitor the entry, lobby, and grounds to be sure that they are kept in good order. If the maintenance crew doesn't share your need for daily sweeping of the entryway, perhaps this is a task that you'll have to assume yourself in the interest of making your clients' first impression a good one. Also, give some thought to the parking situation outside your residence. If it's not self-explanatory, then be sure to alert clients where to park (or *not* to park) when they schedule an appointment.

CLIENT DROP BOXES

Having a client drop-off and pick-up box is an excellent way to make it even more convenient for clients to work with you. You will enjoy the freedom from interruptions (at dinner time, children's bedtimes, when you're working in your pajamas at 6:00 A.M.); your clients will appreciate the flexibility of being able to leave materials for you at any time and pick up completed projects when convenient for them. Boxes or slots may be attached to your door or located in a weatherproof container on your front steps, for example. If you have the space, consider using two boxes, one for "incoming" and one for "outgoing" work. It has occasionally happened to me that one client, not looking carefully, has grabbed two or three envelopes—even those with others' names on them. It has then become necessary to track down and get back the missing files. Anything left in a drop box should be sealed and clearly labeled with the client's name. Files should only be left for clients when they specifically request it, for their convenience, and, naturally, material that is highly confidential should not be left in easily accessible pick-up boxes.

Apartment or condo dwellers face a more complicated situation regarding client drop boxes. If you feel confident in the security of your building, you may be able to create and use a drop box in the foyer, or it might be feasible to utilize the management office. Attaching boxes to your individual unit's door may be possible—though it may not be practical if visitors need to be let into the building by a resident. Perhaps you could consider installing a locked box and giving keys to specific clients. If installing a drop box is not feasible, be sure to investigate and have in place several delivery options such as courier, overnight mail, and Federal Express.

SAFETY ISSUES

You should consider personal security when thinking about establishing a home-based business. You may be alone in your home, meeting with clients you know only through a brief telephone conversation. While nearly 100 percent of callers present no safety issues, on rare occasions you may feel uneasy after speaking with a caller. Here are a few suggestions concerning safety:

- Trust your instincts if a caller makes you feel uncomfortable for any reason.

- Working by appointment only—an excellent practice for a one-person service businesses for a variety of reasons—ensures you will not be surprised by drop-in customers.

- Some home-business owners, particularly women, feel more comfortable not publishing their address in any advertising, using instead a PO box or merely listing their city.

- The longer you engage a caller in conversation about his or her business project, the less likely the chance that there will be a security problem. How many ill-intentioned callers are going to spend ten or twenty minutes discussing a business presentation or brochure with you if they have other ideas in mind? Don't schedule an appointment until you have a good grasp of the client's requirements and feel comfortable inviting him or her to your home/office.

- When working alone at home, consider playing a radio or television in another room to give the illusion that someone else is in the house.

- Work out a prearranged signal with a neighbor so that if you are in trouble, you can easily call for help.

- Give the client the strong impression that you are expecting another appointment "at any minute."

OFFICE ESSENTIALS

Your office arrangement is dependent on your specific equipment and the space you have available. Essentials include:

- Your *main work surface*—as large as possible!

- A comfortable *computer setup*, with appropriate arm and wrist rests to ensure your comfort and health.

- *Client meeting space.* If possible, try to have a separate desk or table for this purpose. It's much easier to keep this one surface clear of papers and ready for clients than to scramble to clean off half a day's worth of accumulated paperwork as a client rings your doorbell. Near your client meeting area, store samples of a variety of DTP projects you've completed. (If possible, get copies of projects after they've been printed so clients can get the complete effect of paper, color, etc.) There should be a good light, a supply of pens and blank Client Information/Agreement forms (for further details and a sample form, see chapter 6), and possibly a stapler, paper clips, and tape. In this area clients will meet with you to discuss their project requirements and again to review, proofread, and possibly assemble their documents. This table is also an excellent place to display brochures, business cards, newsletters, and other promotional materials, along with magazines or other reading materials for clients to peruse in the event they have to wait for you for a few minutes.

- *Storage areas and containers.* As mentioned previously, cabinets or closets are ideal. You will need to keep some materials close at hand, so having a variety of storage options in close proximity to your work area will make it easier to keep order and control over your various projects. Stacking, letter-size trays provide convenient and orderly storage space for paper supplies and client files. Computer disks should be protected from dust and careless handling in a holder that allows easy review of disk titles; wood, plastic, and cardboard disk storage boxes are widely available. Storage containers for pens, pencils, rulers, and scissors offer a great opportunity to add a decorating touch to your office, as a number of creative containers can be used. I frequently use plain gray printer's boxes to store paper, to keep it dust-free and flat.

- *Places for less-used equipment.* Your copy machine can be tucked into an otherwise unused corner. A color printer or fax machine might be placed on a table across the room. I don't recommend that everyone keep a large copy machine and document-sorter in their living room, as I did for several years, but if your office is very crowded, do consider locating rarely used equipment in another area of your home—perhaps a dry basement, spare bedroom, or unused closet.

- *Accessibility for frequently used items.* Your telephone, everyday printer, invoices, active client files, pen supply, frequently used diskettes, paper clips, postage stamps, a stapler, and other daily use items should be within arm's reach.

- *Ample light*—both task lighting and ambient (room) lighting.

- *Sufficient electrical outlets* to allow you to plug in your equipment without having extension cords draped around the room. As noted earlier, installing a few dedicated outlets will be helpful in preventing flickering lights or blown fuses from having too much power drawn from the same circuit. (Copy machines and air conditioners are both power-hungry appliances.) You should also install *surge protectors* (available very inexpensively from electrical or computer supply stores or catalogs) wherever sensitive computer equipment is plugged in. A power surge coming through the electrical wire can irretrievably damage your computer. It's just not worth the risk when the prevention is so easy and inexpensive.

- *Telephone jacks* located strategically around the room. Phones, faxes, and modems all need to be connected.

Although your office is intended for business purposes, it is perfectly appropriate to give it a personal touch. Since you will be spending so much time in your office, surround yourself with colors and objects that give you pleasure—photographs of your children or pets, collectibles, attractive vases with fresh or silk flowers, window treatments that add color and can be opened or closed for light control. My own office is a good reflection of my personal interests—family skiing pictures, numerous pictures of my children, an autographed baseball, a framed photograph of Fenway Park, wallpaper and window trim in restful blue and lavender. I'm also a rather untidy worker, so I've tried to impose some organization with numerous slotted shelves, storage containers, bookcases, and file cabinets.

It's easy to take for granted and not really "see" any room in which you spend a lot of time. Periodically—and particularly before a client's first visit—step back and give your office the once-over. Clearing up clutter is one of the easiest ways to improve any room's appearance. Dusting, vacuuming, and window-washing should be done regularly so that your office reflects a positive and professional image.

HEALTH, COMFORT, AND ERGONOMIC ISSUES

Repetitive stress injury and carpal tunnel syndrome are two types of injuries that have appeared in headlines and generated much discussion around office watercoolers in recent years. Heavy, repetitive computer use can contribute to these injuries, which can disable workers and cause considerable pain and discomfort.

Safeguard your health—avoid these painful and disabling injuries by using common sense and following a few guidelines for computer use. First of all, take frequent breaks to stretch your muscles. Roll your shoulders, flex and open your fists, stretch your arms out and swing them in a circle. Hands and wrists, in particular, are susceptible to this type of injury. Using a computer mouse, with your arm locked in one position and your index finger using a repetitive motion, is a risky activity. If you find your hands or arms frequently cramped or sore, consider trying out a different type of mouse than the standard. There are track balls and "power mice" that allow different and possibly less stressful motions. In addition, wrist and arm rests are available that help you maintain correct position while working. If you experience severe or chronic discomfort, see a doctor for treatment—don't let it linger, thinking it will get better by itself.

Your physical comfort can also be enhanced or exacerbated by your office chair. Sitting too long in any chair can cause discomfort, but you can minimize this by choosing a chair that offers good support and the ability to change height and seat-back angle easily. Keeping your feet elevated on a stool under your desk may alleviate lower back and leg discomfort. Again, as with your hands and wrists, it is helpful to get up and stretch regularly. Take a brisk walk out to the mailbox. Turn on the radio and dance for a few minutes to loosen up your muscles. (Dancing is also a great energizer when you're working late and have run out of steam. Put on something fast and familiar and have some fun!) Even throwing in a load of laundry or vacuuming for a few minutes can be enough to break the repetitive nature of working at a computer or hunched over a desk all day.

Maintain overall good health and flexibility by exercising regularly and keeping as active a lifestyle as possible for someone with a desk-bound job. Your health and energy are irreplaceable—and from both a professional and a personal standpoint, you cannot afford to lose them.

CHAPTER FIVE

MARKETING AND SELLING YOUR SERVICES

> There is no security in life. There is only opportunity.
> — **DOUGLAS MacARTHUR**

Who am I?

I'm a corporate vice president. I'm a restaurant owner. I'm head of a high-school parent organization. I own a print shop. I'm a musician. I edit a newsletter for my professional organization. I'm a bank purchasing officer. I just started my own consulting firm. I am a sales representative. I own a dance school. I'm a building contractor. I run children's art workshops. I own a plastics manufacturing company.

Who am I? ***I am your client.***

Desktop publishing clients can be found in every industry, in Fortune 500 and one-person businesses, in large cities and small towns. To make your business successful, you must create in these various marketplaces an awareness of your business, the services you provide, and how these services can benefit them. And that's what marketing is all about.

Consider, too, that many of your potential clients are not familiar with the term "desktop publishing"—or if they have heard of it, they're not quite sure what it means. Unless you establish your niche market among individuals and companies who are well versed in DTP terminology and procedures, part of your job will be to educate your clients as to just what is involved in desktop publishing. You will also need to use marketing tactics that appeal to individuals with all levels of DTP sophistication.

When planning your marketing strategy, keep in mind that there is a very large market among individuals who have less-sophisticated desktop publishing needs: retailers who need flyers and are delighted when you add graphics; small manufacturers with intricately numbered price lists that are updated regularly; new business start-ups with a desire for professional-looking letterhead yet a limited budget; organizations and associations of all kinds needing a variety of membership materials. This type of client will respond to a different marketing approach than, for instance, a graphic designer who needs a desktop publisher to coordinate text with his graphics, or a large corporation with extensive in-house DTP expertise and a need for an additional resource to handle occasional overflow work. The point to keep in mind is that you need to speak the language of your clients or prospects so that they understand what you can do for them.

In any business, marketing is an ongoing activity. Even when you have established a strong client base and your business is thriving, it's essential that you continue your marketing activities. For a variety of reasons, there is a certain level of client attrition in any business. Companies close or change focus; a project is completed; a business expands to the point where your client needs to hire a full-time desktop publisher; spousal relocation causes another client to move across the country. You'll note that the loss of these clients is in no way related to your business's service, quality, or pricing. But to maintain and increase profitability, you must continually work to add new clients to your roster.

The term *marketing* encompasses a broad variety of activities. Every time you speak to someone about your business or hand out a business card, you are doing marketing. When you write a letter to the editor and sign with your business name, that is marketing. Advertising, direct mail, and cold calling are marketing, too. Your professional image and activities in your business community are all marketing-related.

For greatest success, you should establish a marketing program that includes a variety of activities—some directly sales oriented, some not. Your goal is to raise awareness of your company in your marketplace and then convert that awareness to action (sales).

To ensure the success of your marketing program, the most important factor is that you *do it*—take some action. A perfect marketing plan on paper or in your head stands no chance of being successful! Dedicate a certain portion of your time and your available resources to your marketing efforts. Select activities that appeal to you in each of the areas outlined below, to keep your marketing program going on a variety of fronts. While it's a good idea to challenge yourself occasionally, don't make the mistake of choosing too many activities that are difficult for you. Human nature being what it is, you'll find yourself with an incredible variety of creative reasons for avoiding those tasks. If you hate cold calling, don't do it—or pledge to make one call a week. If you don't enjoy belonging to civic organizations, don't make that the focus of your marketing program. Create a plan that suits your personality and your business, and make marketing a regular part of your business activities.

Marketing may seem an overwhelming task. To make it more manageable, it can be broken down into three essential areas:

- **attracting clients**
- **retaining clients**
- **increasing sales to existing clients**

To achieve and attain success and to keep your business growing, it is essential that you employ marketing strategies in all three of these areas. Let's explore a variety of techniques for successful marketing in each.

ATTRACTING CLIENTS

Naturally, as a new business, attracting clients is your foremost task. It's also the most difficult job for any business. The good news is that your initial task, that of attracting first-time clients to a spanking-new business, will never be as difficult as it is right at the beginning, particularly if you use effective techniques in the other two critical areas—retaining clients and increasing sales to existing clients.

As noted previously, desktop publishing clients can be found in literally any business or industry as well as in the nonbusiness (consumer) marketplace. The broad appeal of desktop publishing services can work to your advantage, in that everyone who is exposed to your marketing message conceivably has a need for your services. Conversely, it's more difficult to form a highly focused marketing strategy unless you are planning to carve out a specific niche in the DTP field. Also, remember that not all of your clients will be computer-literate businesspeople with a good understanding of what desktop publishing is all about. In my experience, DTP clients will call and ask to have something "typed" just as frequently as they will request "desktop publishing" services. In most cases their use of the terminology will not be up to the level that has become your everyday language. Your marketing campaign, then, must be designed to educate as well as advertise, and you must devise strategies to attract clients who may not know exactly what desktop publishing is or may not know that they need it. That said, let's look at ways of attracting new clients.

Advertising

Advertising is a primary means for attracting business. *Yellow Pages* advertising is an extremely effective vehicle for many types of businesses and can certainly lead clients to your door. It's important to appear in the Yellow Pages for several reasons—most importantly, if your competitors appear there, you should too. But Yellow Pages advertising is not the only—or even the most effective—means of attracting new clients. Some new-business owners fondly imagine they can list their business in the Yellow Pages, sit back, and wait for the customers to roll in. Sorry, it's just not that easy! Still, Yellow Pages advertising is an important component to your overall marketing plan.

Begin by reviewing the Yellow Pages directories for your own city as well as nearby areas. Depending on the geographic breakdown of your telephone directories, you may be located in close proximity to towns served by other directories. If you are located in a suburban area with its own phone book, you should also review the large metropolitan directory. See where your competitors are located and the size of their ads. One comforting fact is that large, full-page ads may not necessarily draw the type of clientele you wish to attract. Frequently, prospects looking for quality and a high degree of personal service will call businesses with smaller ads instead of those they perceive as the "giants" in the business.

A business-to-business Yellow Pages may be published in your area and would seem a natural place for desktop publishers to appeal to other business owners. My experience has been that this directory is not widely used, though it may be different in your area. Check around with businesspeople you know in your locality to determine if this might be a worthwhile place for you to advertise.

When reviewing the Yellow Pages, examine all categories that pertain even remotely to desktop publishing. Here are some suggestions:

- desktop publishing
- printing
- typing
- typesetting
- word processing
- graphic design
- computer services
- resume services
- secretarial services

Bear in mind that you need to advertise where your prospects will look. Therefore, based on my experience, it makes sense to consider advertising under "Resumes" and "Typing"—for me, these two categories have consistently pulled the most response. It's very likely that prospects calling with a need to have something "typed" or "word processed" will, in fact, be good candidates for desktop publishing services. With regard to resumes, even if you choose not to offer writing and editing services, your design, formatting, typesetting, and printing expertise will help you gain substantial business in this highly profitable field.

Jan Melnik of Comprehensive Services Plus in Durham, Connecticut, considers word processing and resume services to be "gateways to the more profitable editorial, consulting, writing, and desktop publishing services." She knows that once she attracts clients initially, she can in almost every instance sell some other aspect of her service based on an assessment of the client's needs and a presentation of ways she is able to meet those needs. So even though her specialization is in areas other than word processing, typing, and secretarial services, she continues to advertise under those Yellow Pages headings because the ads garner large numbers of new clients.

After completing your Yellow Pages review and considering the available categories, make a list of preferred categories and ad sizes. It's probable that the high cost of Yellow Pages advertising will prohibit you from fulfilling this "wish list," but it's a good place to start.

Next, call the Directory Advertising business number listed at the front of the book and speak with a sales representative. Crucial information to find out at this point is their *advertising deadline*—usually about three months prior to the annual publication of the directory. Ask for *advertising rate information* as well, and be sure to inquire about *new-business discounts*.

Advertising options within the Yellow Pages include plain line listings, bold listings, in-column ads (1/2-inch up to 3 or 4 inches), and display advertising—eighth page, quarter page, half page, full page. As you might expect, the display advertising is the most expensive—and, as noted above, is probably *not* the most effective for a desktop publishing service. In-column ads allow you to provide significant information in a location that will be seen immediately by readers as they scan the categories. Here is where you gain the advantage of an early-in-the-alphabet business name that will appear toward the top of the category. This is especially important if there are many listings in a category.

With plain and bold listings, you will not be able to include any supplementary information about your business. If there is no strong competition in this category, however, a listing may be enough. Or you might consider adding a line, such as "See our ad under Desktop Publishing Services," if you have placed a larger ad at another location. There is an additional cost for these referral lines.

Color is now available in Yellow Pages advertisements. You may be able to select red, blue, white, and/or green to emphasize your advertising message. Yellow Pages sales representatives will show you statistics on the increased effectiveness of color, but keep in mind that this, too, is an extra cost. If your advertising budget is limited and you have to make a choice,

I recommend a larger black-and-white ad with more information rather than a smaller ad in color.

When preparing the copy for your Yellow Pages ads, stress the benefits and services you provide to clients. My Yellow Pages slogan, "Providing personal, professional service since 1982," emphasizes what I consider the hallmarks of my business: service, quality, and longevity. Give as much information as you can fit and still maintain an attractive-looking ad. Benefits you might mention include speed ("24-hour turnaround"), convenience ("MasterCard/Visa accepted," "easy access off Route I–90"), quality ("we make *you* look good"), and service ("we're committed to your satisfaction"). Product/service listings should be included to give readers a concrete idea of what you can do for them, but don't overcrowd your ad. You may choose not to publicize your address, for security reasons and to discourage drop-in clients. There is usually an extra charge for omitting this information.

At the time you place your initial call, you will be assigned a sales representative, who will visit your office to secure your advertising order. Be sure to request a proof of your ads. You may get the party-line answer—"I'm not sure if we'll be able to get them in time." Be persistent, because having an incorrect ad or one with a typographical error will have a negative effect on your business—for an entire year! (If by chance the Yellow Pages does print an incorrect ad, use this as a negotiating tool when speaking with your representative the following year. You should be able to secure a significant discount or additional ad space to make up for the costs to your business of their error.)

Newspaper advertising, in general, is not the most effective means of advertising for desktop publishing services. An exception is advertising in your local *business journal*—a dedicated local (typically citywide or regional) business newspaper, usually published weekly or monthly. Most often these publications are delivered to office addresses, so your prospects will be seeing your ad in an environment that is conducive to making business decisions. When contacting the advertising representatives for these journals, again be sure to ask about discounted rates for new advertisers. You also might wish to consider placing a classified ad in a small-market *daily* or *weekly paper* in your area. Quite often these prove to be well read by individuals and small-business owners and may provide a steady stream of small assignments. As well, if your market niche is small businesses in your community, a well-read local paper might be an excellent choice as an advertising vehicle.

Radio and television advertisements, because of their relatively high cost and scattershot approach, are not the most effective media for desktop publishing advertising.

Other advertising opportunities will present themselves as you operate your business. When evaluating each possibility, consider the target audience and the value for your advertising dollar. With a modest marketing budget, you simply cannot afford to overspend on unproven forms of advertising.

Marketing studies have proven that prospects need to see an ad numerous times before they act on it. Many businesses get discouraged and discontinue their advertising before it has a chance to work. If you decide to use a print ad, make the commitment to run it long enough to be effective. Don't panic when your first week's ad doesn't draw any business—give it the time it needs to succeed.

Word of Mouth

Word-of-mouth referrals occur when your name, business, and/or expertise are on the minds and tongues of clients and prospects. This is achieved as a result of the combination of all your marketing efforts—advertising, promotions and publicity, referrals, networking, and so on. It's essential, therefore, to keep your name in front of prospects in a variety of ways. Any time you can draw positive attention to your business—through a newspaper article, volunteer activities, idle chat at a neighborhood barbecue, reaction to a DTP piece you prepared, your paid advertising, and so on—you will benefit from your increased visibility to clients and prospects.

It may be difficult to track the effectiveness of this type of marketing, since it often results from a combination of activities. New clients may not even be sure exactly where they learned about you, or their general knowledge may be a result of having heard about you from a variety of sources over a period of time. You will know word of mouth is working when clients say such things as, "I heard about you around town"; "I asked a couple of people who they use for DTP"; "I think I saw something about you in the paper"; or "Gosh, I don't know—your name just came to mind when I needed this work done, so I gave you a call first."

To capitalize on word-of-mouth marketing, take advantage of every opportunity that comes your way to promote your business with people in the community in both business and social/casual encounters. You don't need to be pushy or to talk about your business constantly. In many cases, a conversation will naturally turn to "what do you do?" You should be prepared with a concise statement in response to that question: "I'm in the business of making you look good on paper"; "I help businesses and individuals to develop printed materials"; "I do desktop publishing—I put together words and pictures in documents of all kinds"; and so on. Try to word your reply in a manner that indicates a solution to a problem, so that the person you're speaking with understands how you help businesses and individuals, even if she doesn't fully comprehend the term "desktop publishing."

You are the best possible advocate for your business—you are knowledgeable, enthusiastic, and authoritative. Be alert to opportunities for spreading the word, and you will reap the benefits in increased awareness in your marketplace.

Networking

As a new-business owner, you'll find that one of your best means of gaining new business is through personal contacts. This is known as *network marketing.*

Begin by preparing a friendly letter to send to every person you know. In your letter, announce the opening of your business and give a brief description of the services you will provide and the type of projects you anticipate. Enclose a brochure and several business cards. (Review the section later in this chapter on developing your marketing materials.) Ask these people—your friends and business associates—to refer anyone they know who might have a need for your services. This type of mailing should at least generate a number of congratulatory phone calls from people who were unaware of your business plans, and you should use this opportunity to engage them in conversation about your business capabilities—and ask them about their desktop publishing needs.

Any referrals you receive should be followed up immediately. These are easy calls to make because you were referred by a mutual friend. Gather as much information as you can about the prospect's DTP needs, and then send a follow-up letter and brochure.

Whether or not these initial efforts result in much business, they are doing the job of disseminating information about your business among people who are predisposed to think positively of you and who are quite likely to talk about your business with other friends and associates. This contributes to the "word-of-mouth" marketing discussed earlier.

Continue your networking efforts by joining organizations where you will come in contact with business decision makers. Very likely there is a business association in your city that welcomes new members. Good organizations to consider joining include the Chamber of Commerce, Rotary Club, Toastmasters, and others that are made up of business professionals. The start-up stage of your business is a particularly effective time to join an organization, while daily work is less demanding and you have the time to participate fully in organization activities.

When attending organization meetings, be ready with your prepared statement in response to the "what do you do?" question. It is *expected* that organization members will exchange business information and actively seek networking opportunities. As a member of an organization, you may have an opportunity to volunteer your desktop publishing services for a variety of projects. Again, with your business in its beginning stages, you probably have the time to prepare programs, membership directories, advertisements, etc., for the organization, and doing so will allow you to demonstrate your skills. Be sure your contribution is recognized—preferably with a credit line on every piece you prepare so the recognition continues beyond the bounds of the organization. Let members know you are qualified and are interested in working on similar projects for them. (And be sure to get a printed sample to include in your portfolio—more about this later in the chapter.)

Another method for getting to know business decision makers in your community is to take an active part in organization activities. Carla Culp (CLCulp & Associates, Edwardsville, Illinois) has this to say about her participation in the Rotary Club in her community: "I get a much higher return on my annual investment in Rotary (dues and meals) than I do for the same amount I spend on Yellow Pages advertising. I look forward to our Wednesday lunch meetings and enjoy opportunities to work with different people on projects where I get a chance to showcase my abilities or to step into the public eye for a while. (Sounds kind of selfish, but that's how I get most of my work!)"

The concept of networking involves a give-and-take relationship. In addition to seeking referrals for your services, you will meet others with whom you can do business. Patronizing their businesses is a good way to cultivate referrals for your own.

Another form of networking is to establish mutually supportive arrangements with related businesses. This is also a good way to defuse perceived competition. As a new desktop publishing entrepreneur, you might approach secretarial service and resume businesses in your area and discuss how your services can complement theirs: They can refer clients with more complex DTP needs, and you can refer callers who simply want word processing, or who need resume writing. Everyone wins with this kind of cooperative arrangement—you, the other business owner, and the client. (Additional information on vendor/subcontractor relationships appears in chapters 2 and 6.) This type of networking works best among businesses in somewhat related fields that will be likely to attract clients who may also need your services. Naturally supportive relationships for desktop publishers include word processors, graphic designers, printers, marketing consultants, and service bureaus.

Client Referrals

This is quite likely the *most effective* form of marketing you can do—and it's free! It does, though, relate directly to the second part of our three-pronged marketing effort: retaining clients. Satisfied clients will stay with you and will refer others to you.

But is there anything you can do to promote or actively solicit client referrals? Yes!

- First, *ask for referrals*. This can be accomplished in several ways:

  In general conversation with your client. ("By the way, if you know of anyone else who might be able to use our services, I'd certainly appreciate the referral.") This is usually most effective immediately after a client has expressed satisfaction with a job you have done.

  As a formal request. Anna Callwood (Bac-Up Business Services, Boston), sends a thank-you card after a client's first use of her company's services, thanking the client and requesting, "If you're not pleased with our service, tell me; if you are pleased, tell a friend." This approach has been successful in increasing referrals to her business.

  As part of a newsletter or other client communication (more about these later in the chapter)—a brief mention to the effect that "satisfied clients are our best source of new business; we greatly appreciate your referrals!"

- Second, *thank and reward referring clients*. In your newsletter, you may wish to publicize a "referral reward"—a dollar amount or percentage discount for every referral. When you complete a job for a referred client, always send a thank-you note to the referring client. Consider developing a thank-you certificate that earns your client a discount on future services. If you can, return the favor by sending referrals to your client's business. These tactics will ensure that making a referral is a satisfying process for your client.

The importance of referral marketing cannot be overlooked. Clients who are referred to you by sources they know and trust are already sold on you and your services. They have heard glowing reports of you from their friends or colleagues. With these clients, service and satisfaction are doubly important. Any lapses will not only affect your new client relationships but, you can be sure, will get back to the original referring clients as well.

Cold Calling

Cold calling refers to unsolicted visits to businesses to introduce yourself and explain your services in hopes of securing these businesses' desktop publishing work. Although cold calls can also be made by telephone, within the context of this section I am referring to actual visits to potential clients.

One of my first cold calls, thirteen years ago, resulted in a mutually supportive, personally enriching, and still-ongoing business partnership.

Having said that, I also want to say that I dislike making cold calls and almost never make them; nor do I think they are a particularly effective form of marketing for desktop publishing services. They are time consuming, and in many cases it may be difficult to make contact with the actual decision makers in the business.

Let me tell you the story of my happy experience. In the winter of 1983, having been in business for only a few months, I gathered up my typing sample book and my infant daughter and went to call on a local printer. I was extremely fortunate in my choice, as this shop turned out to be owned and operated by a husband-and-wife team who were committed to providing high quality and outstanding customer service. When they discovered that my business could help their customers and learned that I shared their priorities, we started working together steadily. In return, I used their shop for my printing needs (which were rather limited at that time). When, several years later, I began to use desktop publishing technology, they were willing to give me a chance with some of their typesetting work. My own printing needs had expanded, and I was extremely pleased to have a high-quality printing source. My increasing interest in design and layout coincided with the arrival of the printers' two sons into the business. They were convinced of the solid future of desktop publishing and began to give me more complex design projects. The alliance worked because of the happy convergence of our needs and capabilities, reinforced by our similar business commitment and personal style and strengthened by open and honest communication.

The success of this early cold call quite naturally inspired me to make similar calls on other printers in my area. It was evident to me that printers and desktop publishers form a natural partnership—particularly printers who do not have their own DTP equipment in-house. My subsequent attempts to develop alliances with printers were somewhat successful; I developed several relationships that were more sporadic than the one described above but lasted for a number of years.

With this outstanding example of cold-calling success, why then do I not recommend it as a primary means of attracting new clients? Let's analyze the reasons my effort was successful:

- The timing was right—at the time of my visit, both business owners were able to spend a few minutes chatting with me, and at that time they were in need of supplementary typing services.

- I was prepared with a sample book that demonstrated my proficiency.

- We established a mutual rapport right from the beginning. They loved my baby (well, who wouldn't?), and in fact my bringing her turned out to be an advantage.

- We shared a similar commitment to customer service and high-quality work.

- My capabilities grew as their needs expanded.

You'll note that over most of these items—the timing, the rapport, the similarity of commitment, the simultaneous business growth—I had no control. I was prepared, and I was professional, but those qualities alone were not responsible for my success.

In cold calling, there are many variables over which you have no control. When you visit a company, will the decision maker be available to speak with you? Does the company have a current specific need for desktop publishing services? Will you be able to establish a rapport? Will the company's growth be in the same direction as yours?

If you enjoy calling on prospects and are skilled at engaging people in conversation, by all means add cold calling to your marketing plan. To increase your chances for success, be prepared with a sample book or portfolio of your own materials. (There is more information on developing your marketing materials later in this chapter.) Be sensitive to time constraints. Use the visit as a means to get acquainted and to share a small amount of information about your company. If you detect interest, ask to schedule a follow-up visit to go over your capabilities and their requirements in more detail. Whether or not you secure a follow-up appointment, send a brief "thanks for your time" letter and additional information in response to any needs you were able to detect during your short visit. Don't expect cold calling to result in an immediate sale. Consider it another way to get the word out about your company.

Cold calling is time intensive and requires you to be away from your office, so factor these considerations into your decision about how much of it to do.

To increase the effectiveness of sales calls, combine them with direct mail (see next section), followed by a telephone call to schedule an appointment. Your call then moves from "cold" to "warm"—and maybe "hot," if the prospect has a definite project in mind. On these prequalified sales calls, you can make a much stronger sales pitch, since the individual knows a bit about your business and has agreed to meet with you to discuss it.

Direct Mail

As with other marketing efforts, an effective direct-mail campaign requires an investment of time, energy, and money. Studies have shown that a minimum of four direct-mail pieces is required before the average prospect responds.

There are two kinds of direct mail we will consider. The first is a four- to six-part campaign sent to a large mailing list and requesting these prospects to get in touch with you. The second is a smaller, more targeted, more personal approach, which you follow up with a phone call to the prospect.

Your plan for a large mail campaign should include four to six different, coordinated pieces, sent once a month to the same mailing list. You can purchase mailing lists or develop your own from local phone directories and business-association membership lists. Mailing to a person instead of just a company name will increase the chances your mailer will be read.

To increase the response rate, each of your pieces should include a *call to action*—a reason for the prospect to respond. Offer an incentive—10 percent off your first project, five free color prints—to encourage response by a specified date. And don't forget to include a "P.S." in any letters you send. Research has shown that postscripts are nearly always read, and they offer a great chance to reinforce your message or repeat an offer. And since they're often read first, make sure that they're worded in such a way that the prospect is curious to find out what the rest of the letter says.

Your direct-mail campaign might include some or all of the following:

- An introductory letter describing your business services and enclosing a brochure and a business card
- A flyer promoting one specific facet of your business—scanning, color printing, customer satisfaction guarantee, monthly "special," etc.
- Your regular client newsletter
- An eye-catching postcard
- A second letter summarizing your capabilities and the services you provide

By the end of your campaign, prospects will have had four to six communications from you. In addition, it is likely they will have noticed your company name from some of your other marketing activities—a news story in the local paper, an advertisement in a business journal, your name in the membership directory of a civic organization, your listing in the Yellow Pages. You have set the stage for prospects to remember you and communicate with you when they have a need for your services.

If you receive no response after your four to six targeted mailings, merely add these prospects to the mailing list for your quarterly newsletter or other regular mailings. Periodically, as your list gets too large, you may purge people and businesses from whom you've had no response.

To execute the second type of direct-mail campaign, develop a targeted list of businesses that you feel have a strong need for desktop publishing services. This type of mailing requires that you write to an individual, so you may have to make a phone call to each company to find out the name of the person responsible for outside desktop publishing, for coordinating printing, for handling design, etc. Write a letter to these individuals outlining your services and specific benefits to their organization. Enclose a brochure and business card, and close your letter with an indication that you will follow up by phone in hopes of scheduling an appointment.

When you telephone these individuals, try to ascertain whether there is a present or anticipated need for your services. If you are unable to schedule a sales visit, ask if they would be interested in receiving occasional mailings from you to stay informed about your business. If the answer is positive (and it usually will be), add the name to your prospect list for direct-mail campaign number one, sending all but the introductory letter, and keep the name on your newsletter mailing list once the campaign is concluded.

A direct-mail campaign is an excellent vehicle for a desktop publisher to demonstrate creativity and the ability to produce effective, attractive documents. Make sure your mailing pieces are a good reflection of your strong DTP skills. I've had clients call and ask me to produce for them a newsletter, postcard, etc., "just like yours." Seeing my own effort, they could visualize their message being conveyed in the same way.

As with print advertising, direct mail requires a certain amount of repetition to be effective. Don't make a halfhearted attempt by preparing one direct-mail piece and then giving up when it produces no results. Direct mail is an investment—be sure to do it thoroughly so that you realize the payback.

Publicity

In its simplest form, publicity refers to stories about you in the paper. Publicity is different from paid advertising. By its very nature as a news vehicle, it is more credible than advertising. It is also something over which you have limited control.

Newspapers welcome press releases and rely on them for part of their news coverage. In particular, small local papers will frequently print press releases verbatim, allowing you to actually write the news story about your business. Larger newspapers are more likely to edit press releases or write their own stories, based on the press-release information and a follow-up interview.

To be effective, a press release must contain news. Starting a business is news. So is the announcement of a new service offering. Winning an honor or award is a perfect excuse for a press release. Press releases are an excellent way to capitalize on any volunteer leadership positions you assume. Offering a free service to the community will practically guarantee your release is printed. A summary of your business capabilities can be included in a newsy press release but is not sufficient for a story on its own.

Begin your press release with contact information (your name and telephone number) and an indication that it is for "immediate release." Write a succinct headline, and then begin the article with the most important news value of the story. The first paragraph or two contains the news information; additional paragraphs provide other details of your business and also contact information for readers wishing to follow up. (See the sample press release for suggested format and content.) Your news releases should usually be sent to the newspaper's business editor.

A more effective form of publicity is a news story, prepared by the newspaper, focusing on you and/or your business. To get such news coverage, it is up to you to bring your story to the editor's attention. After becoming familiar with the typical content of a particular publication, develop a few "angles" for interesting stories. Each individual and every business has a story to tell. Your job is to package the "hook" for presentation to the news editor. Consider the following possible news angles—they may or may not apply to your unique situation:

- Mother of twins starts home-based business (*human interest/job trends angle*)

- ABC Desktop Publishing wins design award from Adobe Corporation (*prestigious award for local company*)

- Lottery winner plans to use funds to start own business (*wouldn't we all like to have this angle to propose!*)

- Corporate downsizing brings success to flexible DTP firm (*capitalizes on current trends*)

BLUE SKIES
Desktop Design

175 Maple Village Row
Springfield, MA 01119

Tel. (413) 555-8585
Fax (413) 555-8586

FOR IMMEDIATE RELEASE

Contact: Christine Taylor
555-8585

LOCAL BUSINESS OWNER TO SPEAK AT
NATIONAL CONFERENCE

Christine Taylor, president of Blue Skies Desktop Design in Springfield, will present a major conference session on "Networking for Success" at the Independent Desktop Publishers Association's annual spring conference. Taylor, who founded her business in 1985, has been at the forefront of the desktop publishing field and is an acknowledged industry expert. She is a frequent speaker on topics relating to desktop publishing, design, and document preparation for both industry and general audiences and has contributed numerous articles to small-business and desktop publishing publications.

In her presentation Taylor will use as examples the networking relationships she has formed with numerous businesses and individuals in the Springfield area. Blue Skies Desktop Design, which specializes in creative graphic design, also offers clients networked services for printing, writing and editing, word processing, marketing, and distribution of a variety of corporate and promotional materials.

In addition to her membership in the Independent Desktop Publishers Association, Taylor is an active member and current vice president of the Springfield Chamber of Commerce and also belongs to the Springfield Rotary Club, the Maple Village Business Association, and the Springfield–Maple Village Kiwanis Club.

Taylor offers no-fee speaking services to local community organizations. For an outline of suggested topics, or to discuss graphic design or desktop publishing needs, contact Blue Skies Desktop Design at 555-8585.

- Local, one-person DTP company serves clients around the world *(another trend—the ability to service clients no matter where you or they are located, due to advances in electronic communication)*

- Local business owner "wrote the book" on desktop publishing *(significant accomplishments of locals are always of interest)*

The idea is to come up with some unique, newsworthy circumstance that applies to you, then package this information so that an editor perceives its news value. An effective approach, once you've developed your idea, is to telephone the editor, introduce yourself, indicate that you have an idea for a story he/she might find of interest to the publication's readers—and then ask if he/she has a few minutes to talk with you about it. If the answer is no, schedule a time for a follow-up call, or offer to send a letter. Then refer to this conversation when you make the follow-up call or send the proposal letter.

In these instances you would not write the story; the editor or a writer will conduct an interview and develop the story themselves. You may have the chance to review the article for accuracy before publication, but more likely you will not see it until it appears in print, frequently accompanied by a photograph. As you might imagine, feature stories are of outstanding value in increasing community awareness of you and your business. (Be sure to mention your business during an interview, even if the focus is on a non-business-related topic.)

If the editor is not interested, don't be discouraged—wait a few months, then call again with another idea. News publications need a constant stream of interesting articles.

Television and radio also offer opportunities for publicity. Television requires a strong human-interest angle or some truly startling news, something that will present well visually. (The lottery-winner idea would probably apply.)

With radio, your best bet may be to offer your services as a guest on a business-related talk show. Establish your credibility and knowledge in a proposal letter to the producer. It helps to be familiar with the show so you can speak knowledgeably about how you envision contributing to their format.

To summarize, a publicity/public relations effort can produce out-standing bottom-line results for your company—for free! I highly recommend including some aspects of a publicity campaign in your over-all marketing strategy.

RETAINING CLIENTS

Studies consistently show that it is many times more expensive to attract new clients than to continue providing services to the clients you have already worked to gain. Therefore, it makes sense to keep your clients happy. The two key elements to customer satisfaction are *quality* and *service*. If you provide an outstanding level of each, your clients will have no reason to go elsewhere. If you fail to retain your clients, you will significantly increase your costs of doing business—and thus reduce your profitability.

The importance of quality cannot be overstated. No marketing or advertising effort can be successful if your work does not live up to its promise. You must do good work, and do it consistently. You must be committed to—even a bit obsessive about—the quality of your work. Strive to *exceed* your clients' expectations. Outstanding quality is the first reason clients will continue to bring their work to you.

Service is the second crucial component to client retention. As the business owner, you have the power and flexibility to do whatever is necessary to ensure customer satisfaction. You should be totally invested in the happiness of your clients because it will result in the success of your business. Good service is expected; exceptional service is noticed and appreciated. Always keep in mind that "the customer is king" (or queen). Clients are the reason you can pay your bills and earn a good living from your business. They are the ones who provide the positive feedback that rewards your creative efforts.

Quality and service are conveyed by your attitude as much as by actual deeds. Your favorite responses to clients' questions should be "Yes!" "Of course!" "I'd be glad to!" Never make clients feel that what they are asking is burdensome. Never tell them you "don't do" something. Be interested in their needs and offer your help wherever possible. Be prepared with a list of vendors and other high-quality businesses to which you can refer your clients for additional work beyond the scope of your capabilities. Better yet, take on the responsibility for all aspects of a client's project, working with your subcontractors to deliver the final product. Make it easy for your clients to work with you.

By committing yourself to quality and service, you will gain a business reputation that will go a long way toward ensuring success. You will also increase the likelihood of gaining referrals from satisfied clients.

And how does all this quality and service translate into profit? After all, we're in business to make money—and if we don't make money, we'll soon be out of business. As noted in chapter 2, as a small business you cannot compete solely on the basis of price unless you are willing to accept longer working hours and/or lower profitability. Instead, distinguishing yourself by your exceptional quality and service allows you to charge a premium rate, due to the added value you provide to the client.

Consider this: If you are providing a truly exceptional level of quality and service and, at the same time, charging extremely low rates, you may very well be the busiest desktop publisher in town. At the same time, you will no doubt be overwhelmed by client requests and feel resentful of the time you are spending to provide this great product and service if you don't feel fairly compensated. You may feel your clients are taking advantage of you. But it's not the clients' fault—as Ann Landers says, no one can take advantage of you without your permission. If you are in this situation, you have three choices: 1) maintain the status quo and continue being overwhelmed and resentful; 2) reduce the quality and service you provide so you can increase the volume of your work and, hence, your profits; 3) increase your rates so you can continue to provide a high level of quality and service and be fairly compensated. It seems obvious that the third choice will yield the most beneficial results—for you *and* your clients.

Because of the flexibility and control you can exert over all facets of your business, you as a small-business owner are particularly well suited to focusing on quality and service as the distinguishing components of your business strategy. By doing so, you give clients a reason to do business with you and to *continue* doing business with you.

An extension to your quality and service focus is the way you handle problems, complaints, and client dissatisfaction. These incidents, hopefully rare, are a real test of your commitment to customer service. Being so intimately involved in your business, as both owner and production worker, when faced with a problem or complaint you may feel personally attacked, become defensive, and try to focus the blame elsewhere. To avoid turning a small problem into a very large one, try to focus on the *solution* to the problem. Depending on the nature of the problem and the ease of solving it, you might offer to redo portions of the work for free, speak to the printer about redoing the job at a reduced rate, or devise a creative way to hide the problem area. In these interactions, try to promote a cooperative teamwork atmosphere so your clients feel you are truly on their side. Helpful suggestions can be made without any admission of responsibility on your part, if in fact the client is responsible. (Having clear-cut policies and a signed policy agreement with your client, as detailed in chapter 6, is an excellent business practice to follow so that responsibilities and obligations of both you and your client are clearly understood.) And if the error is yours, accept the responsibility immediately, ensure your client is satisfied to the best of your ability, and consider it a learning experience.

Client Appreciation Program

Plan to implement a "client appreciation" program that focuses some of your marketing resources on existing clients—beginning with the first client who walks through your door. Make this program an integral part of your business activities so it doesn't get lost in the rush when your business begins to increase. Some elements of this campaign might include:

- *Client thank-yous*—Send a brief, hand-written thank-you note to each new client, expressing appreciation for his or her business and the hope that you can continue working together. This very simple and inexpensive strategy is especially effective because so few businesses actually do it. Additionally, as part of your overall client communications effort, consider sending out one or two mailers a year that merely express thanks and appreciation. Appropriate times of the year to send such a message include Thanksgiving, Valentine's Day, and the anniversary of your business or the date your client started working with you. This communication might be in the form of a greeting card, a hand-written note, or a postcard. You might want to include a certificate offering a discount on future services as your way of saying "thanks."

- *Client-satisfaction survey*—When conducting such a survey, ensure respondents' confidentiality so that you will get back honest responses. These replies very definitely will be helpful in determining clients' true level of satisfaction and possibly refining your service offerings. You might include a survey, along with a prestamped envelope for return, with your client's work at the conclusion of your first project together. Or you could mail it to the client within a few days of completing a project. You will get an immediate response if you use a telephone survey—but in this case, you should not conduct the survey yourself, since very likely the client will not feel comfortable expressing dissatisfaction. A disinterested third party is the best person to conduct such a survey; perhaps a college student, retired individual, or parent at home with small children would like to take on this project for an hour or two each week. Have a prepared script, and have the person taking the survey write complete responses to the questions asked. A client-satisfaction survey, whether completed in writing or by phone, should involve no more than five or so minutes of your client's time.

  Before instituting a client-satisfaction survey, prepare yourself to receive complaints, criticism, and other expressions of dissatisfaction that you probably never heard about when working with the client. Instead of taking offense or getting defensive, look at this information as a golden opportunity to fix the problem areas so they don't become ongoing sources of client dissatisfaction.

- *Client gifts*—a token of appreciation for their business. You might consider giving an inexpensive gift to all clients—a coffee mug, coaster set, pen, or other imprinted item that will constantly remind them of your business. For your best clients, a gift during the holiday season is appropriate. I've given such items as fruit or gift baskets, wine, chocolates, books, flowers, and dinner certificates. These are fun to select—you will enjoy matching the gift with the specific client.

- *Client hospitality*—an opportunity for you to celebrate some accomplishment, such as an anniversary of your business, and share your hospitality with the clients who have made it possible. A wine-and-cheese reception or holiday open house are relaxed events that will be enjoyable no matter how many, or how few, clients show up.

Client appreciation can be simple or elaborate, low-cost or expensive. Select methods that suit your personality and your business relationship with the client.

While it's essential to attract new clients, too many businesses seem to take them for granted once they've come through the door. Making each client feel valued and appreciated each time you work together will assure a high level of client retention—crucial to the success of your business.

INCREASING SALES TO EXISTING CLIENTS

Having attracted your clients, and retained them through quality, service, and appreciation, you should also strive to extend your relationship with them.

Selling to existing clients occurs as a result of communication: You find out what your clients need, and they learn of additional services you provide. Clients who come to you for letterhead design may not be aware that you can also handle the printing of their letterhead—unless you tell them. Clients for whom you design newsletters will not know that you also write newsletters—unless you let them know. And so on. Be alert to opportunities to offer additional services related to your clients' projects.

Learning about your clients' needs requires that you engage them in conversation. It's that simple, and that enjoyable. Ask your clients questions about their projects. People love to talk about themselves! Most clients will respond to your genuine interest and enthusiasm. Having learned what some of their additional requirements might be, it's a simple matter for you to suggest ways that you can continue to work with them. Ask them: "Would you like me to get some printing quotes for you?" "I can have my service bureau take care of the separations—do you want paper or film?" "Do you have a mailing service lined up, or would you like me to handle that for you?" With questions like these, you are making it easy for clients to continue working with you. You show that you know what their needs are, and you offer solutions. You have become more than simply a desktop publisher—you are now a problem solver!

The more you can promote these kinds of exchanges with clients, the more they will come to see you as a complete resource—and the more work they will entrust to your care. Candace Battle Rhodman of Business Services Etcetera, Nashville, Tennessee, sums it up this way: "I try not to make a sale with a client; I try to provide them with a solution that leads to a sale. My goal is to establish a relationship with the client that will be long lasting."

As noted in chapter 2, it is appropriate to mark up vendors' charges to compensate yourself for your liaison services. Thus, even if you are not doing the work yourself, you will increase your profitability.

Learning about your clients' needs through conversation will also alert you to the possibility of adding profit centers to your business. You may notice opportunities to offer additional services that seem to be desired by many of your clients. This may require you to invest in new equipment or acquire training in a new function but will benefit your business by improving its capabilities. As an example, when I noticed my clients increasingly asking about color output (report covers, overheads, etc.) and learned through conversation that they found color materials to be more effective, I investigated color printers and bought one for the purpose of providing these materials directly to my clients instead of continuing to use my service bureau for this purpose. Not only did this increase my billings, it also positioned me in the forefront of desktop publishing—I acquired a color printer just as color was becoming more talked about and slightly more commonplace in most business offices. Adding this profit center was beneficial for both my clients and me.

An additional way to inform clients of your capabilities is through formal communications—letters, postcards, and especially newsletters. Keeping in touch with your clients even when they are not actively involved in working with you will serve as a reminder of you and your business.

Following are some suggested methods for staying in touch with your clients on a regular basis:

- *Informal notes.* Sending a brief, handwritten note to an individual client is appropriate for a number of personal and professional accomplishments and occasions—a promotion, election to a leadership position, a new baby, a new home. Also, a brief note just to say "thanks for doing business with me" will be appreciated. For this purpose, you can order through your local printer a box of small note cards, perhaps imprinted with your name or your business name.

- *Phone call.* A brief, friendly phone call to a client is an excellent way to keep in touch and may also be the catalyst he or she needs to get a pending desktop publishing project back on track. You can merely call to inquire how things are going for them—say you came across their name during the course of your day and were just wondering how they were doing. Or follow up on a project you did for them—ask how their presentation went, or whether the brochure was effective. Your purpose should be to show interest in their business and foster the friendly relationship you have developed.

- *Holiday greetings.* The Christmas/Hanukkah season is the traditional time to send holiday greetings. Instead of a standard card, try designing an eye-catching postcard that you can laser print on preprinted, perforated postcard stock with a holiday theme. (See the Appendix for a list of specialty paper companies.) All your mailings offer a great chance for you to show off your design and layout expertise in real-world applications that will be sure to catch your clients' attention. Other holidays offer opportunities to stay in touch, as well—in fact, a holiday greeting sent at Thanksgiving, Valentine's Day, Fourth of July, etc., will stand out more than a Christmas card because it most likely will not be one of a crowd.

- *Client-satisfaction surveys,* described previously, can be mailed out to clients following their first project with you or periodically, as a means of ongoing communication. Be sure to inquire about other areas where they might envision using your services—clients may suggest new profit centers or additional services in an area you hadn't considered.

- *Postcards.* I love postcards. They are quick and easy to prepare, inexpensive to mail, and always read. They are an ideal vehicle for a brief message using strong visuals to get the point across. They can be fun, lighthearted, and more playful than a more formal newsletter or letter. Use your graphic-design talents to create innovative postcards that promote a specific service or product or convey a message of appreciation.

■ *Newsletters.* As the owner of a desktop publishing firm, you are in an ideal position to use a client newsletter as a marketing tool. First, you have the technology and the expertise to make it look great. Second, very likely it's the type of project you would enjoy doing for your clients; sending your own reinforces your expertise. Third, it's enjoyable to use your creative abilities for your own project, after spending most of your time preparing work for your clients. Newsletters can be sent as often as monthly, but my experience shows that quarterly is a better schedule. You don't want to overwhelm your clients with mailings, and also it's less burdensome for you to create each issue when it's only every three months. Numerous formats can be utilized. When creating my initial newsletter, I tried to strike a balance between economy and creativity: I wanted my clients to be impressed with the quality and appearance of my newsletter, but I didn't want to break the bank producing it. For that reason I decided not to use an odd paper size, a four-color printing process, or bleeds. I started out with a black-and-white newsletter on colored stock but later redesigned it to accommodate two-color printing on white or gray stock. To minimize writing time and printing costs, I chose to use a one-page format, printed on both sides, with the "news" of each issue covering one side and the back side available for a product and service listing and mailing panel (it's a self-mailer, requiring no envelope). Each issue promotes a specific service (e.g., scanning, presentation graphics, newsletter production), with an informative article about the particular service and how it can benefit the client. Frequently I will feature a new service I am offering, such as color printing. Other informative articles give tips relating to my areas of expertise, such as spelling, grammar, writing, or organization. A personal-greetings section begins each issue, and the page is rounded out with vacation notices, business news, and other items that will be of interest to my clients. (See the Appendix for additional resources on how to prepare a client newsletter.)

If you elect to create a newsletter, it's imperative that you keep to your publication schedule. A newsletter is a soft-sell approach that increases its effectiveness with the regularity of its publication.

News and Views

from Best Impression • 9847 Catalpa Woods Court, Cincinnati, Ohio 45242 • (513) 792-0030

SUMMER 1994   Volume 3, Number 3

Greetings

"...summer's lease hath all too short a date."
Wm. Shakespeare

In my childhood, summer seemed to last forever. My brothers and sisters, neighbors and I spent from early morning till well past dark outside, getting sunburned, mosquito-bitten, filthy and exhausted—only to start anew the next morning. It never seemed to rain, except in wild, exciting thunderstorms that caused the electricity to fail and made cooking in the fireplace a necessity! No doubt these idyllic, nostalgic memories were far different from my mother's point of view. I know that the yearly family camping trip was always a delightful adventure—but now, as the "mom," I'm daunted by the amount of work I know it would entail!

Nowadays, Shakespeare's sonnet rings truer to me. Already my summer calendar is filled with travel plans, relative visits, ambitious goals of book-reading, strawberry-picking, gardening. Although it's busier than my recollections, I hope I'll be able to make some memories this summer that are just as satisfying as the ones from my childhood. And I hope you can, too.

Louise Kursmark

Word Power

While preparing for participation in the annual Blue Ash adult spelling bee, I came across many words whose meanings (never mind spellings!) were completely obscure. Diligent effort paid off, however — our team, the "Killer Bees," came in second out of 35 teams. Here are a few interesting words I discovered:

PRESBYOPIA *n.* The inability of the eye, especially with advancing age, to focus sharply on close objects. *Many of my friends have begun to experience presbyopia, as evidenced by their purchase of magnifying glasses from the drugstore.*

SCHOTTISCHE *n.* A round dance in 2/4 time. *Did they dance a schottische at the celebration ball?*

VERTIGINOUS *adj.* 1. Turning about an axis. 2. Affected by or likely to cause vertigo. *Meredith enjoyed several vertiginous rides at the amusement park.*

SUMMER SPECIAL
We Do Brochures Right!

Tailor-made brochures offer a perfect solution to many business requirements for delivering effective messages to multiple audiences.

At Best Impression, we can help you design, write, and produce a brochure in any quantity (dozens or thousands). We're happy to answer paper, printing and mailing questions and help you pre-plan so that your brochure includes all the necessary elements.

Through September 15, 1994, we'll give you **20% off** the creation and development of a brochure. Let's discuss the unique possibilities in store for your business!

Professional News

● In addition to being a frequent contributor to various business and professional publications, Louise Kursmark has recently been named Contributing Editor to *The Word Advantage*, a quarterly newsletter for secretarial service and desktop publishing professionals.

● Thinking of preparing your resume? Not sure where to start? A two-session course on resume and cover letter preparation will be offered in early fall through the Blue Ash adult education program. Louise Kursmark, who will be the course instructor, will draw upon her 12 years' experience writing and preparing thousands of resumes. You can learn to do it yourself... or contact Best Impression and we'll do it for you!

Vacation Notice

Best Impression will be closed the following dates this summer:

July 12–17 **Professional Conference San Francisco**

Aug. 10–14 **Vacation**

Please plan ahead and contact us to coordinate your requirements in plenty of time.

News and Views is designed, written and produced by Louise Kursmark, Best Impression, Cincinnati, Ohio • © 1994 Louise Kursmark • Printed on recycled paper.

BEST IMPRESSION
9847 Catalpa Woods Court
Cincinnati, Ohio 45242

NEWS AND VIEWS

from

BEST IMPRESSION

9847 Catalpa Woods Court • Cincinnati, Ohio 45242 • (513) 792-0030

desktop publishing and design, word processing
and related services for businesses and individuals

at your service... 792-0030

- desktop publishing and design
- computer graphics
- tape transcription
- telephone dictation
- mailing list storage and updates
- fax
- laser printing
- typesetting
- photocopying
- mailing
- pick-up and delivery
- rush service

- newsletters
- brochures
- flyers
- manuals
- proposals
- presentations
- overheads
- business correspondence
- repetitive letters
- price lists
- catalogs
- resumes

It's important to stay in regular contact with clients, particularly those who use your business only sporadically. You want to be sure they think of you when they have a desktop publishing need. Your communications keep your name on their minds and also serve to educate them as to your capabilities.

DEVELOPING MARKETING MATERIALS

With all of this communicating going on—newsletters, postcards, letters, press releases, publicity—you will need to develop printed materials that identify and provide information about your business and are a good demonstration of your desktop publishing and design skills.

Your Professional Identity

While developing your business name (see chapter 3), you no doubt did some experimenting with a logo or simply setting your business name in various typefaces. Perhaps you even printed stationery, envelopes, and business cards. If you are happy with the image you've established for your company, you can proceed immediately to develop additional identity pieces, as described below.

At this point you should have a pretty clear idea about the image you want your company to convey. If you haven't yet created a distinctive logo or appearance for your business, you should do so now. Emphasize the qualities that match your business focus—*professional, creative, inexpensive, businesslike, daring, powerful, cute, deluxe*—whatever is appropriate for your business. Now it's time to put on your designer's hat and experiment with different ways to get that message across. Try using graphics, different typefaces, and varying positions on the page. (It's a good idea to develop a logo, which is a strong visual identifier for your company.) If you don't feel confident in your design skills, now's the time to call on a graphic designer for professional assistance. To save money, engage a designer to create only the logo itself, which you can then integrate into all your materials.

You may also wish to develop a slogan that encapsulates your business philosophy. You can play on your company's name (Best Impression—We help you make *your* best impression!; Advantage Business Services—Giving you the advantage) or some particular strength of your business. Here are a few real-life examples: "Helping you look great on paper" (WordSmith, Rockland, Massachusetts); "Your one-stop support shop" (Park Avenue Secretarial Service, Dayton, Ohio); "We are your solution provider" (Business Services Etcetera, Nashville, Tennessee); "Helping businesses do business" (Bac-Up Business Services, Boston, Massachusetts). If you do develop a slogan, use it on all your printed materials so that its message becomes linked with your company name in the minds of your clients and prospects.

Let's examine some things you'll want to consider in developing your professional-identity materials:

- *Letterhead.* Be sure to include all your contact information—business name, address (mailing address and physical address, if different), telephone and fax numbers, e-mail address. Don't forget your slogan, if you have one. Your name should be displayed, along with your title. Since it's your company, you can call yourself anything you wish. Titles you might consider include "President," "Principal," "Owner," and "Designer." I personally favor "President" because it conveys your authority and role as the decision maker.

  When designing your letterhead, keep in mind the kind of stock you plan to print it on. Your paper choice, too, can do its part in conveying your company image. Consider using something a bit unusual to help your materials stand out. Make sure, however, that you don't select a paper that photocopies poorly, as any time your materials are copied, your image will be damaged. Check whether your paper choice is available in a variety of weights so you can, if you choose, keep a consistent image by using the same stock for your business card, brochure, and other pieces you may develop. Also, as noted in chapter 3, consider printing a quantity of your letterhead on inexpensive white paper for your own office use—memos, invoices, forms, etc. Consult with a printer or two about paper choices, colors, etc., as you refine your design.

  If you are using color, you will realize some savings in printing costs if you are able to print all your materials—letterhead, envelopes, labels, invoices, brochures, etc.—at the same time.

  When your letterhead design is completed, develop a complementary layout for an envelope, including just your business name, logo, and mailing address.

- *Mailing labels.* When sending pages flat, you will use large envelopes to which you can affix an identifying label. You also may wish to label folders or envelopes containing client work. These large mailing labels, usually about 4 x 3 ½ inches, offer another opportunity to carry forward the look you have created for your business. An alternative would be to have matching 9-by-12-inch envelopes printed up with your logo and return address.

- *Brochure.* This important component includes detailed information about your business and the services you offer. You should include your business philosophy, slogan, an indication of your commitment to quality, and other pertinent information that will give the reader an accurate and detailed picture of your business.

    A brochure is often a prospect's first close look at your business. A strong design that communicates your message effectively will be doubly effective—containing both information and an example of your desktop publishing skills.

- *Business cards.* For its small size, a business card carries an oversized responsibility for conveying your business message. There are numerous ways you can use your business card for marketing purposes: Enclose a few with every invoice or client letter for retention and referral purposes. Always have a stack on hand in the office, ready to give to clients who think they may know someone who could utilize your services. Send one out along with a brochure and letter in response to a phone inquiry. Hand out business cards freely at organization meetings, and be prepared to take home a pocketful yourself.

    Since your business card is so widely used, you should make sure it is doing its job as well as it can. In addition to your name, business name, telephone numbers, addresses, and slogan, consider adding a list of business services you provide. This becomes particularly effective if your business name is not descriptive or if you find many clients and prospects unclear on the concept of desktop publishing. If the card becomes too crowded, you can print a two-sided card or even a fold-over card, which gives you nearly four times the available space as a standard business card. Extend your business image by printing in the same color ink on stock similar to your letterhead, but heavier.

A word about *preprinted designer papers*, available by catalog from specialty paper companies (see the Appendix for a list of resources): Although these papers are attractive and are an excellent resource for various desktop publishing projects, I caution against using them as your main corporate identity for several reasons. First, not all papers are available in every format you'll need now and in the future (stationery, envelopes, mailing labels, business cards, postcards, brochures, etc.). Those that are available in all formats tend to be the more popular designs, thus increasing the chances that "your" materials will be seen representing someone else's company. Also, consider the possibility that the company may discontinue printing the design at any time, leaving you in the lurch when it comes time to reorder stationery. (In many cases, though, companies give notice when a specific design is going to be withdrawn, thereby giving you the opportunity to stock up on the items you use.)

Another consideration is that, as a professional desktop publisher, you may find the designs inhibit or clash with your own design work. The preprinted papers work best with simple text formatting that is complemented by the papers' usually elaborate and colorful designs.

That said, I must admit that I used predesigned papers for my own company image during the transition of my move from Massachusetts to Ohio. I felt I needed to present an attractive, professional, colorful appearance yet didn't want to invest in a complete set of professional-identity materials until my new address and phone number were definite. Also, producing brochures on my laser printer a few at a time gave me the opportunity to refine and revise my service offerings in my new location.

Preprinted designer papers can also be used very effectively for certain client projects and may closely match the client's needs, especially where a big, colorful impact is desired but only a small quantity is needed.

DEVELOPING AND USING A PORTFOLIO

In addition to your own professional-identity materials, you should develop a portfolio of examples of various projects you have completed. This is an excellent tool to use during client presentations to demonstrate the quality and variety of your work. Also, when you are meeting with vendors or making cold calls, your portfolio will give a good representation of your work and will also contribute to your professional image.

In your portfolio, include samples of a variety of projects. Try to obtain final-version, printed copies of your materials so that important factors such as color and paper choice will be demonstrated. If that's not possible, laser-printed originals may be used instead.

When you're starting out, you may find you don't have enough samples of work. This is where volunteer activities become useful. Offer to produce a specific piece at no charge for an underfunded organization, and then add that piece to your portfolio. You will be gaining valuable experience, helping a worthwhile cause, and improving your marketing materials, all at the same time.

Consider adding to your portfolio a brief description of the scope of the work you performed. For instance, you might describe a brochure in this manner: "Three-fold brochure developed for charitable organization on a very limited budget. To accommodate cost restraints, utilized an inexpensive but unusual paper and edited clip art rather than creating original art. Brochure increased direct-mail response more than 20 percent over prior mailer." Develop similar synopses for other pieces that you feel require explanation or may have involved unusual circumstances.

You may also wish to include in your portfolio testimonials written about you by satisfied clients. Testimonials, usually unsolicited, are highly believable and can back up particular claims that you've made in your sales presentation. If you find you're not getting testimonials from clients, try this: When clients compliment you on a particularly effective piece of work, ask them to put it in writing. Tell them you're developing a portfolio of testimonials and would love to add theirs to it—"especially with a challenging project like this one that came out so well." It's also easy to request a testimonial in lieu of payment for any volunteer desktop publishing projects you've done.

When presenting your portfolio to a client or prospect, it's likely that you will not want to include all your samples. This may be too overwhelming to the client and end up decreasing the effectiveness of your presentation. Instead, choose those samples that closely match the client's image or specific project and also demonstrate your versatility.

To keep all these materials in order, consider using a three-ring binder with clear plastic inserts into which you can slip the appropriate samples. Better yet, large leatherlike portfolios with handles and zippers can accommodate larger samples and are easier to carry along to client meetings. These large portfolios usually have clear plastic inserts which, like three-ring binder pages, will protect your samples and can be mixed and matched according to the occasion.

Showing samples of your work can also be an effective sales tool within your office. A neatly arranged bulletin board displaying various projects is an easily updated attention-getter that also adds color and originality to your decor. If you have bookshelves that are easily accessible, use them to display samples encased in picture frames. A binder containing samples can be displayed on the table where you meet with clients—be sure to label the cover clearly ("Samples—Please take a look!") so that clients don't hesitate to open the book and review your work.

Meeting the challenge of marketing and selling your services requires an ongoing combination of a variety of efforts. Even when your business becomes busy and successful, it's important to maintain a marketing focus so that these essential activities don't get overlooked in the rush of day-to-day work.

CHAPTER SIX

GETTING THE WORK DONE

Heigh-ho! Heigh-ho! It's off to work we go!

— **THE SEVEN DWARFS**

In addition to doing the work of desktop publishing, you will have the responsibilities of organizing the work flow, setting priorities, keeping deadlines, maintaining easily accessible client information, and establishing systems that enable you to track and analyze your business. To prepare for the day when you become overwhelmingly busy with numerous projects and clients—and that day *will* come!—you should start off on the right foot by putting these organizational systems in place from day one. There are many systems that work; the trick is using them consistently so that they become the engine that drives your business operations, humming along quietly in the background and making it possible for you to concentrate on production work.

In this chapter we'll look at various systems for organizing your business and also discuss the management of daily activities. Specific forms that I've developed for gathering, grouping, and tracking data will be presented, along with examples of how to use them. When preparing your own organizational tools, bear in mind that no system is effective unless it's used. If you model a form on one in this book but find you're not using it because it seems needlessly complex and burdensome, then by all means simplify it! Conversely, if you find you're always looking for a specific bit of information, then add it to your form. Customize everything here so it fits—or use nothing at all, if that suits your style. There are no hard-and-fast rules to organizing and operating a business. Use what's presented here to guide you in creating a unique system that allows you to get a handle on the facts, figures, and work of *your* business.

ORGANIZING AND SETTING PRIORITIES

My key to daily organization is an active and informative *Project Schedule*. I've gone through many permutations of this form in my own business, from simple, handwritten "to do" lists in full-page and half-page format, to elaborate tracking and organizing forms, and finally to its present incarnation, a simple table created in my word processing program. This file stays open at all times and serves as a constant reminder of items scheduled for the day.

Your Project Schedule should reflect *all* assignments, both immediate and long term, and their due dates. Projects should be entered on the schedule as soon as they are received, to reduce the possibility that they will be overlooked or forgotten. This sounds like a simple matter, but life is not usually very orderly! The workday is frequently interrupted by phone calls bringing new and revised assignments; completing one stage of a project requires schedule updating to start the next phase; projects get bumped and need to be rescheduled; deadlines change. Developing the discipline to record your project information immediately will result in an effective, accurate schedule and a less stressful work environment.

A typical list of projects to be done includes some with immediate priority and others with deadlines down the road. Items to be done "today" should be grouped at the top of the list, followed by those that are less urgent. Also included on the schedule are tasks that need to be done relative to your own business operations, such as preparing your quarterly newsletter or completing your monthly billing. Sorting action items into groups with descriptive subheads may make it easier to organize the day's activities with just a glance at the schedule. During the course of an average day, the schedule will change many times as you complete some jobs, add others, and change priorities based on phone calls, client requests, and other factors.

Let's take a look at a sample Project Schedule and discuss how activities throughout the day result in changes and adjustments.

PROJECT SCHEDULE

CLIENT / PROJECT	TIME SCHEDULED	DUE DATE/ APPOINTMENT	NOTES
THIS WEEK			
Pat Connors Overheads	3 hours MON	WED 8 a.m.	Fax proofs before printing transparencies (color)
CPM Consultants Training manual	2 hrs MON, 3 hrs TUES, 2 hrs WED	THURS deliver by noon	First draft: edit existing manual, redesign
Priority Printing Misc. typesetting	2 hours TUES	TUES p.m.	
Martha Entwhistle Resume	1 hour TUES	WED 9 a.m.	Typesetting only; no editorial
Bill Thomas Marketing brochure	2 hours WED	FRI 9 a.m.	Copy provided; just typesetting & layout
Allied Art Supplies Price list update	1 hour WED	FRI	
Marlene Rogers Logo design	2 hours THURS	next MON	
Acme Plastics Corp. Catalog	3 hours FRI	next week	
Direct mail campaign stage 2: send postcard	1 hour FRI	mail on MON	add to list: Ken Carlton, VP Corp. Ops., Smith Bros., 1110 Main St., 45211
NEXT WEEK			
Anthony Logan CD booklet	5 hours	before the 15th	CD and J-card All text on disk
ABC Corp. Business forms	4 hours	end of next week	
Anne Darwin Copy onto disk	.3 hr.		2 versions brochure PageMaker/IBM
FOLLOW UP/MISC.			
Order transparencies for color printer	MON	TUES by 3 p.m.	specify next-day delivery
Word Pros Acme catalog text	MON	TUES	
G Graphics—color seps, Acme catalog photos	TUES		their courier should deliver Wednesday
Priority Printing Ed's business cards		needs by THURS	
NOTES			

- Don't schedule work time Friday p.m.—Matt's in-school birthday party at 1:00, then client meeting with Prince Advertising at 3:30
- Chamber of Commerce mtg. 8 a.m. Wednesday—talk to Nancy about babysitting

Imagine you are starting work on Monday morning with the Project Schedule outlined on the previous page. Glancing at the schedule, you see that today you need to complete a first draft of Pat Connors' overheads, which need to be faxed for approval before final output. You must also order blank transparencies today so you'll have them tomorrow—Pat will be picking up the final copies at 8:00 A.M. on Wednesday. Today you also plan to begin work on CPM's training manual and should check with Word Pros on the status of the text they're preparing for your use in the Acme catalog.

While only five hours of work are "scheduled" for today, remember the "75 percent rule" (chapter 3)—only 75 percent of your time will normally be spent in billable hours, with 25 percent allotted to nonbillable tasks. Booking the entire 75 percent (i.e., six hours out of an eight-hour workday) limits your ability to accept lucrative rush jobs or squeeze in a project for a very good client. Also, as a home-based business you have the option of not working the traditional eight-hour, 9:00-to-5:00 office day. Working a nontraditional schedule offers many advantages, and flexibility in structuring your work time is one of the joys of owning your own business. If you choose, for instance, to spend every Thursday afternoon volunteering in your child's classroom, be realistic about the billable work you can perform that day. If your schedule calls for significant production work during evening or early-morning hours, make sure to allow enough time in your daytime schedule to make phone calls and get answers to questions that occur during the hours when you may not be able to reach clients.

Getting back to our example, since Monday is a typically busy phone day, you complete only four hours of the five you have scheduled. In response to phone calls and faxes, you put immediate priority on a resume revision for an out-of-work client who has an interview scheduled that afternoon; you spend half an hour on the phone with a good client discussing color-output options for an upcoming project; you respond to a bevy of phone calls from new and existing clients and schedule an hour-long client project meeting on Thursday afternoon. In addition, to complicate your schedule further, the overheads take four hours to do instead of three—during the course of the morning, Pat faxes several additions. You postpone beginning work on the CPM manual, hoping that you can make up the lost hours on Tuesday. Before ending for the day, you review your Project Schedule and establish new priorities for tomorrow's activities.

On Tuesday you get up early and begin work at 6:00 A.M. with the goal of spending a few uninterrupted hours on the CPM manual. You make excellent progress and decide to continue working on it while you're on a roll. Taking a lunch break, you reexamine your Project Schedule and realize you've promised Priority Printing's typesetting this afternoon. You complete and deliver it, taking the opportunity to ask if the business cards you brought in last week are ready. They are, so you're able to cross that reminder off your follow-up list after calling your client to inform him that the cards are ready. Later in the afternoon you hear from Pat with a few minor changes, and after making the revisions, you print out overheads on the transparencies you found in your drop box, delivered by your office supplier. You realize you didn't follow up on the text input you left with Word Pros, so you place a quick call and are assured that you'll have the material by the end of the day on Wednesday. After dinner and some family time, you head back to your office for an hour of relatively undemanding typesetting on the resume that will be picked up at 9:00 on Wednesday morning. Before heading to bed for some well-deserved rest, you review your Project Schedule to prepare yourself for the next day.

Keeping your Project Schedule on the computer makes it extremely easy to add items, revise dates, change priorities, and in general keep the list neat and truly reflective of project status. When I used a handwritten schedule, I found myself rewriting it several times a day in an attempt to keep order in the midst of the chaos that usually reigned. Also, when kept on a computer, the list can contain as many items as necessary, whereas a handwritten schedule is confined to the space available on the page.

I prefer to keep my Project Schedule on my word processing program as opposed to a spreadsheet or a dedicated scheduler/calendar. Since my word processor is in daily use, the file can be left open for immediate reference and frequent updating.

The Project Schedule is also handy for jotting brief notes about small tasks to be done—for instance, in the example above, "add to list Ken Carlton, Smith Bros." is added to the notes column across from the reminder to prepare and mail direct-mail campaign #2, a postcard. Perhaps Mr. Carlton called with a general inquiry, or you may have contacted him in response to a networking referral. You may not have had your database easily accessible when you spoke with Mr. Carlton so, if you're like me, you jotted down the note and his address on a small scrap of paper. Transferring this information to your Project Schedule will prevent the information from being lost while reducing the clutter on your desk!

Set up your Project Schedule in a way that is easy for you to use. Whether it is handwritten, computerized, or made up of repositionable Post-it notes, it must be conducive to being revised easily and frequently. And it is vitally important that you do your part to keep it up to date by entering all project status changes and additions as they occur.

You'll note that in the scenario presented above, sufficient lead time was built into most deadlines to allow for some slippage. Due to the vagaries of a business that provides services to multiple clients, changes to your schedule are inevitable. As well, while you can estimate the time required for a particular job (and you will become increasingly proficient at this as you gain experience), once you actually begin the work, you may find that the job takes longer than planned. You may have overlooked an element of the project; perhaps when placing the client's graphics you find that their quality is poor and they need to be rescanned; it's possible the client neglected to inform you of an additional job requirement; or maybe one of your subcontractors slips his or her deadline by a few hours or a day, thereby pushing back your own time frame. It's far better to expect things to take longer than estimated, and build a cushion into your schedule, than to constantly be running behind deadlines because you failed to anticipate these circumstances.

When first discussing projects with clients, be sure to find out their deadlines, and notate your schedule with specific dates and times when the work is due. With a large or complex project, you may have several interim deadlines as well as a final project due date. When projects in a draft stage are being reviewed by clients, you'll need to add a follow-up item to your list so that you keep on schedule for completing the project.

Over the years I've found that many friends and colleagues in the industry share with me a strong deadline orientation: We can do whatever it takes, whenever it needs to be done (such as 3:00 A.M.), to complete a project according to a client's deadline. But trouble arises with those projects that have no firm deadline. When a client says, "Oh, there's no hurry—whenever you get to it," that project inevitably gets put at the bottom of the list and never moves up to priority position until it becomes an urgent matter. I've tried establishing false deadlines and time schedules to work on such projects, but I have trouble fooling myself! It's possible that with a less hectic schedule I'd make more progress on those nonurgent projects, but I have a suspicion that this trait is a factor of my personality and work style—the very quality that makes me so good at meeting a deadline somehow prevents me from taking action when no deadline is imminent! For this reason, I always ask clients to give me at least an indication of when they would like the project. That sets up an expectation in both our minds as to when it will be done, and it does help get the work scheduled and completed.

Calendar Options

While it's possible to combine a calendar with your Project Schedule, I find it more convenient to keep a portable day book for recording appointments—though I do make a notation in the Project Schedule to reflect significant events that will affect my productivity. My preference is for a week-at-a-glance calendar, showing seven days on a two-page spread in a 5- by 7-inch spiral-bound notebook. You might prefer a full-page-size notebook, an erasable wall calendar, a comprehensive organizer like the Franklin Day Planner, or some other calendar format. Whichever method you choose, be sure to record every appointment—including the appliance repair person, a haircut, or your children's doctor visits—so that you don't inadvertently schedule a client visit at a time when you will be occupied with other activities or, worse, out of the office altogether. An advantage to a portable calendar is that it can be carried with you to meetings and functions you attend away from your office, allowing you to schedule completion dates, follow-up visits, and other events with confidence.

GATHERING AND MAINTAINING CLIENT INFORMATION

Another important organizational challenge is record keeping with regard to individual clients. Let's examine ways to collect, maintain, and utilize pertinent client information.

Client Database

A client and prospect database containing all pertinent information should be started with your very first client or targeted mailing list. With database software you can create numerous fields so that the file becomes a complete record of your client's activity with your business. Whatever you want to know or track about individual clients and your client base as a whole should be contained within the database. You can then sort, review, and analyze the data in a variety of meaningful ways. For instance, recording how a client heard about you will allow you to determine how much of your business comes from referrals and whether a particular form of advertising is effective. You may be able to generate invoices directly from your database. This is certainly convenient, as the program will automatically insert the client's name, address, billing terms, etc., and will also keep a record of ongoing billing for individual clients.

Contact-management programs contain similar information to a database and also allow you to schedule events—follow-up calls, direct-mail marketing, and other notations specific to each individual contact (client or prospect). They also permit you to merge client data with a memo or invoice for immediate communications.

Even if you choose not to use database or contact-management software, at the very least you will need a client/prospect list in mailing-label format for continued communications and marketing efforts.

An alternative to using a database is to maintain client-information files in your word processing program. While you will not be able to use sorting, grouping, mailing-list conversion, and other database functions, you will be able to maintain detailed files on specific clients. And, since your word processor will likely be in daily use, you will be able to access client files immediately in response to a phone call or to check on past billing history, for instance.

The following hypothetical Client Information File displays information that would typically be included in either a database or a word processing client file. The level of detail included would naturally be greater for a good, frequent client and less for a one-time or occasional client.

Your client database should be updated each time you work with a client. Phone numbers and other contact information should be

CLIENT INFORMATION FILE

CLIENT NAME	ADDRESS(ES)	TELEPHONE NUMBER(S)

Evan Dougherty, Director
Human Resources
ABC Corp.
	OFFICE: 4975 Broad Street,
	    Cincinnati 45123
	HOME: 1887 Smith Street
	    Cincinnati 45242
	E-MAIL: edough@abc.com
		555-1000 ext. 49
		Fax 555-1001
		(513) 555-0101
		
		PAGER: 513-400-4000

PROJECT SUMMARY

Date	Project/Notes	Amount Billed
6/15/95	Personnel manual Design and layout	$1,149.75
7/31/95	Revisions	$85.00
8/5/95	Company application forms	$495.00
10/12/95	Recruiting brochure Editing and layout	$374.25
11/7/95	Revisions/printing Priority Printing: $350 Cream linen/brown ink (PMS)	$422.25
12/10/95	Holiday greeting card	$225.00

ADDITIONAL INFORMATION

- Referred by Jane Swanton (resume client, 3/95), new Purchasing Manager at ABC Corp.
- Sent new baby card, 8/1/95 (Meredith Leigh)
- Incoming president, Chamber of Commerce (Jan. 1996)

reviewed with the client and revised as necessary. When the project is completed, add a summary of the project and the amount billed. This running account gives you an instant snapshot of client activity over a period of time.

Client Information/Agreement

This form is filled out the first time you meet with a client. It records such essentials as client name, address, phone number, and other contact information; how the client found out about your services; a description of the project, the due date and estimated cost (if the client needs to know this up front); an acknowledgment of your policies; and the client's signature. The completed form should be stored in your Client File, if you maintain one, or filed alphabetically with other completed forms.

Client File

Established the first time you work with a client, a Client File contains the original of the signed Client Information/Agreement along with completed Project Trackers and invoices. You may also wish to keep a final print-out of each client project.

Maintaining an individual file on each client is an easy matter for some businesses, particularly those with fewer, larger clients. Some DTP businesses, however, particularly those that are generalists offering a wide variety of services, may find they are servicing many clients with small jobs on a very sporadic basis. In this case, it may be more sensible to maintain one file with completed Client Information/Agreements, filed alphabetically, and only create separate files for those clients whose volume of work merits it.

Policy Statement

It may not be practical to obtain a client's signature on a Client Information/Agreement each time you work together, particularly as you develop an ongoing relationship. Yet it's important that clients have a thorough understanding of your company policies—especially with regard to payment terms and proofreading. For this reason you might want to prepare a brief summation of your company's policies and present it to the client the first time you work together. If you do use a separate Policy Statement, the Client Information/Agreement should include the client's acknowledgment that he/she has received a copy of your policies, has reviewed them, and understands them. With the client's signature attesting to his or her acceptance of your policies, you have strong documentation

professional desktop
publishing services

LOUISE M. KURSMARK

9847 Catalpa Woods Court
Cincinnati, Ohio 45242

513-792-0030

CLIENT INFORMATION/AGREEMENT

Date _____

Client Name _____

Company _____ Address_____

Telephone: Office_____ Home_____

Project _____

Source_____

Details/Special Instructions_____

Deadline/Estimated Completion Date_____

Estimated Cost $ _____

$ _____

$ _____

Total $ _____

Less Deposit _____

Est. Balance Due _____

Cash, checks and credit cards (M/C, Visa, Discover/Novus) are accepted.

The above estimate is provided to the best of our ability following initial review/consultation. Final invoice is based on actual project requirements. Significant differences between estimated total and actual requirements will be discussed with the client prior to completion of the work.

A nonrefundable deposit of 50% of the estimated total is required. Completed work cannot leave the office until full payment is made, unless alternative billing arrangements have been made in advance. Additionally, client agrees he/she is responsible for full payment of total charges for work agreed to even in the event the client determines he/she no longer needs the work and/or does not return to pick up the work. Final proofreading is the responsiblity of the client. The client hereby agrees he/she had an opportunity to review the materials and approve their entire content prior to delivery and/or reproduction.

The client's signature below certifies understanding and agreement with all of the statements of this document.

Signature _____ Date _____

to support your position in the event of a disagreement relating to one of your policies.

Even with clients' signed acknowledgment and acceptance of your policies, it's a sound practice as you work with clients to remind them of their responsibilities (such as proofreading) and obligations (such as payment terms and conditions). This ongoing communication reduces the chance that your client will forget your policies or take your services for granted. For instance, when a client calls to say the brochure you prepared is "all set to go to print," you might reply, "Great! So you've completed a final proofreading and didn't find any errors or changes?" The client might respond by saying, "Well, I assume you've checked it . . . . I just glanced at the changes from the first version." At this point it is an easy matter to remind clients that although you have carefully reviewed their material, it is their responsibility to perform final proofreading, and once the job is at the printer's, it's too late to change or correct anything. A friendly reminder, backed up by the client's awareness and acknowledgment of your policies, will reduce potential conflicts and provide you with the authority to implement your policies.

You might also consider creating a *Client Sign-Off Sheet*, which requires the client's signature and acceptance of particular aspects of a job. In some cases, particularly with a complex project, it's wise to have the client sign off on several interim steps; this assures that both you and the client are in agreement on the work that has been done so far and authorizes you to proceed to the next step. Sign-off sheets are most frequently used when clients authorize you to have their materials printed. The signature acknowledges the client has proofed and approved the final material (attach a copy to the sign-off sheet when filing) and authorizes you to have it printed (state printing details such as quantity, paper, colors, and cost). This protective measure is usually used by businesses or individuals who have gotten burned in the past—perhaps a client claimed he never saw the final copy and refused to pay the printing bill, or was outraged at the final cost of a project even though it had gone through numerous client-specified revisions. The procedure can be handled very professionally, as a part of your normal business procedures, and it does promote accountability by the client.

LOUISE M. KURSMARK

9847 Catalpa Woods Court
Cincinnati, Ohio 45242

513-792-0030

BUSINESS POLICIES

Our number-one business policy at Best Impression is a commitment to customer satisfaction. We want you to be delighted with the documents we produce and the process of working with us.

We feel your satisfaction will be enhanced if we communicate with you thoroughly so that you know what we're going to do and also what your responsibilities are. We do not want you to have any surprises when working with us—except, perhaps, at how good we can make you look!

OUR RESPONSIBILITIES

We will design and produce documents so that they meet your needs and expectations. We'll listen to you and ask questions so that we understand the message you're trying to convey. We understand that an effective design must contribute to the purpose of your document.

We will provide an estimate if requested. We will honor our price quotes (provided the work requirements are as specified). We will complete your work in the time promised.

We will accept your text on disk if it conforms to our guidelines, as detailed in an available guideline sheet. Otherwise, we will re-enter the text and charge you at our normal word-processing rate.

We will be responsive to your phone calls, faxes, and other communications.

We will carefully review and proofread all materials before presenting them to you for your review.

We will correct and revise all documents once (unless otherwise specified) without an additional charge. Additional corrections and alterations will be charged at our normal hourly rate.

We will prepare accurate invoices conforming to any initial agreement or our standard hourly rates and will submit these invoices promptly.

YOUR RESPONSIBILITIES

You will communicate with us fully, freely, and honestly so that we can execute our work to meet your needs and expectations.

You understand that additional job requirements given to us after our initial agreement may result in increased costs or time needed to complete the job.

You will do your part to keep projects on schedule by being responsive to our questions, reviewing materials promptly, and understanding that significant changes and alterations after a project has begun will likely delay the completion date.

You will take responsibility for proofreading your materials. Once you have done so and give final approval, any changes or corrections will incur an additional fee. Correcting a laser-printed original will involve a minor expense; correcting high-resolution or color output will involve a greater expense; correcting quantity-printed materials will involve a significant expense.

You agree that you are responsible for all print shop costs once you have given approval to print and specified a print order.

You agree to pay our invoices fully and promptly, in conformance with the payment policies specified on our invoice.

UNDERSTANDING/ACCEPTANCE OF POLICIES:

UNDERSTANDING/ACCEPTANCE OF POLICIES:

For Best Impression: Signature   Date

Client Signature   Date

STRUCTURING WORK TIME

It is essential to create productive work time amidst family activities, business-operating requirements, client meetings, phone calls, household emergencies, errands, pick-up and delivery of work, and a myriad of other interruptions that occur during the course of a typical day in a home-based business. Work of a creative nature, like many desktop publishing assignments, demands a period of concentrated activity; an interruption in your train of thought can drive that bright idea right out of your head. I've found my ability to concentrate in the midst of chaos has actually *decreased* over the years I've been in business. Perhaps being the mother of very young children forced me to work productively even with constant interruptions, distractions, and uncertainty as to how long the work period would last. (My daughter, my firstborn, was famous for twenty-minute naps . . . just long enough for me to get seriously into a project.) As the children have gotten older and are gone from the home for predictable and lengthy periods of time, I find it necessary to do creative or difficult work when I'm alone. This might be during school hours (although I still have to deal with the interruptions of client visits and phone calls), early in the morning, or—usually—very late at night. There are *no interruptions* from 10:00 P.M. to 1:00 A.M.! And if I can function until 3:00 A.M., that can be a very productive work time.

Your own schedule will, of course, fit your unique situation. Be sure, though, to create for yourself good-sized blocks of time that you can devote strictly to production work. Save those jobs that require less concentration for times when you will have to deal with distractions and interruptions. Using your Project Schedule to keep track of obligations such as bills to pay, newsletters to send out, supplies to order, and other tasks associated with running your business is a good way to ensure they are not forgotten; then dash off a task or two whenever you have a few spare minutes—waiting for a complex file to print; on hold with software support; when a client is running a bit late for a scheduled appointment.

Sometimes it's difficult to track billable time when there are frequent interruptions. A brief phone call (one or two minutes) would not necessitate "stopping the clock," but eight or ten two-minute phone calls or one fifteen-minute call would be a different matter. Keeping a piece of paper near the phone for jotting down stopping and starting times can help you assess whether you will need to make adjustments in billing time. Another method is to review each work session as it is completed to determine if all time can be billed legitimately to your client, or whether you need to make allowances for interruptions. Some production workers like to use a clock with stopwatch features that they press each time they're interrupted, then press again when resuming work. For others, maintaining an overall awareness of productivity during a work session is sufficient and allows them to make appropriate adjustments to billable time. If you start out with the more casual methods but find your time requirements regularly exceeding what you've estimated, consider instituting more formal time-keeping procedures, at least until you develop an overall sense of how productive you really are. Creating your own standards for typical jobs will be helpful as well (see chapter 7), so you'll know how long something should take and can review your activities if your times are considerably different.

KEEPING ORDER

Keeping order in a paper-intensive business like desktop publishing is always a challenge—more so for some of us than for others! I admit that I'm not a naturally neat worker. I seem to survive—even thrive—in my own orderly chaos, and in the throes of daily work my desk becomes covered with client files, books, notes to myself, mail awaiting a response, catalogs, and the like. I make a concerted effort to restore order upon the completion of every project and at the end of the day, and I find this is helpful in preventing the chaos from getting unmanageable.

It's also important to have in place a strong organizational system that, like the Project Schedule, you habitually implement:

- Client work, as soon as it is received, is placed in a file folder and labeled with the client's name. File folders come in the standard manila color as well as numerous bright and pastel colors—you might like to match your folder color to your office decor or logo.

  I laser-print sheets of small labels with my logo, business name, and telephone number, leaving enough room to write the client's name when I affix the label to the folder.

Alternatively or in addition to a folder, you may wish to use a 9-by 12-inch white envelope and have printed on it your *Project Tracker* form (see next item). Using an envelope helps to keep miscellaneous small papers from getting lost and is a good place to store client disks with no risk that they'll slide out. Having all the job specifications written on the envelope also helps to keep these details well organized and clearly notated.

- A Project Tracker is put into the folder with the client's materials, the folder is placed in the in box, and the assignment is added to your Project Schedule.

  The Project Tracker form is used to keep a running account of time spent on the project, particular job specifications, questions or problems that arise, and other information pertaining to the work at hand.

  Projects of short duration will typically require only one or two entries in the tracking log. Many DTP projects, however, are complex and continue over a period of days, weeks, and even months. Using the Project Tracker form to record the time spent and a summary of the work will enable you to respond accurately to client questions. In addition, preparing a detailed invoice that encompasses all aspects of the work is a breeze, with this information taken directly from the Project Tracker.

- Each time you work on an assignment, pull out its folder and enter the date and time in the first column of the Project Tracker. At the end of the session, the form is used to note the ending time, summarize your activities, and record billing information.

- When the project is completed, use the Project Tracker to prepare an invoice (or add to the client's statement for monthly invoicing, if appropriate). Project Trackers for completed assignments should be filed in the Client Folder.

- When clients pick up their work, they keep the file folder, leaving your office with tidy and attractive packaging. You'll find that these folders will serve as ongoing advertising, keeping your business name in front of clients. The readily available phone number also makes it an easy matter for clients to call you again, even years later, when they take out that project for revisions.

professional desktop
publishing services

LOUISE M. KURSMARK

9847 Catalpa Woods Court
Cincinnati, Ohio 45242

513-792-0030

PROJECT TRACKER

Telephone _____

Client _____

Project _____

Details/Specifications _____

_____

_____

_____

_____

Due Date/Time _____

☐ Call Client   ☐ Appointment Scheduled _____

DATE/TIME	WORK SUMMARY/NOTES	HOURS	RATE	TOTAL

Notes/Questions/To Resolve

_____

_____

_____

_____

PROJECT TRACKER (CONTINUED)

Client _____

Project _____

DATE/TIME	WORK SUMMARY/NOTES	HOURS	RATE	TOTAL

Notes/Questions/To Resolve

_____

_____

_____

_____

B E S T IMPRESSION
professional desktop
publishing services

LOUISE M. KURSMARK

9847 Catalpa Woods Court
Cincinnati, Ohio 45242

513-792-0030

PROJECT TRACKER

Telephone _____555-4800_____

Client _____Chris Hawkins, Anthem Real Estate_____

Project _____Marketing brochure_____

Details/Specifications _____8 1/2 x 11, three-fold_____
_____black plus spot color (PMS 072 Blue) — coated card stock (white)_____
_____qty.: 1000_____
_____scan logo, use other graphics as appropriate_____
_____bold & attention getting but not too playful_____

Due Date/Time _____Oct. 1: final printed brochures. Fax interim drafts to Chris for review._____

☒ Call Client   ☐ Appointment Scheduled _____

DATE/TIME	WORK SUMMARY/NOTES	HOURS	RATE	TOTAL
9/15 10-10:45	Client meeting: review brochure copy, make recommendations re: formatting	.8	$48	$38.40
9/18	Scan Anthem logo		1 @ $15	15.00
9/18 10-12:10	Design/layout: faxed to Chris	2.3		110.40
9/20 4-4:35	Revisions: faxed to Chris and discussed printing quotes	.7		33.60
9/24 3:15-3:40	Final copy approved; met with printer	.4		19.20
9/29	Courier delivery of finished brochures			12.00
	TOTAL TIME	4.2	$48	$201.60
	ADDITIONAL SERVICES			$27.00

Notes/Questions/To Resolve _____Include home tel.?   YES—555-4761_____
_____Does she have an e-mail address?   NO_____
_____She'll pay printer directly_____

Invoices

Client invoices are normally prepared upon the completion of every job, although with some clients you may establish monthly billing, and with some jobs interim billing is appropriate. The amount of detail contained in an invoice will vary depending upon the client's needs and the complexity of the project. For work done on an hourly basis, you should identify the project and itemize the services provided and the appropriate charges. If you are working on an assignment for which you have negotiated a per-project fee, merely bill the appropriate dollar amount and reference the project agreement. ("For desktop publishing services rendered per agreement dated 12/12/95—$1,200.") Later in this chapter is a discussion on estimating and billing projects and establishing a project agreement.

Monthly invoices should provide details of each individual project for which you provided services during that month, to assist clients in tracking their costs.

It's quite likely that you will, on occasion, provide services at no charge for clients, for a variety of reasons. Clients will appreciate this, so be sure to let them know what they're getting. Add an item to their invoice—for instance, "Rescan of logo—no charge."

Generating an invoice on your laser printer is a simple task, although you may wish to design a preprinted invoice format. Hard copies of invoices can be retained in your Client Folder (with the appropriate Project Tracker forms attached) or, alternatively, merely as computer files.

Be sure to include on your invoices your name and mailing address and a statement of your terms, according to your preestablished policy: "Payment due within ten days." "Terms net 30 days. Unpaid accounts will be assessed a finance charge of $1\frac{1}{2}$ percent per month (18 percent annually)." If your invoice is directed to a company, be sure to include the name of the individual responsible for working with you. Any purchase-order number assigned to the project by the client company should also appear on the invoice.

While the invoice is often presented to the client simultaneously with the completed work, you may find it advantageous to delay preparing and sending the invoice until you are certain the job is complete. Last-minute changes can occur regularly, for any number of reasons. Hav-

BEST IMPRESSION

professional desktop publishing services

LOUISE M. KURSMARK

9847 Catalpa Woods Court
Cincinnati, Ohio 45242

513-792-0030

INVOICE

Date ___October 2, 1995___

TO: Anthem Real Estate
1895 Main Street
Anytown, OH 45000

Attn: Chris Hawkins

Purchase Order No: CH5595

DATE	DESCRIPTION OF SERVICES	AMOUNT
9/15 - 9/29/95	Desktop publishing and design services; marketing brochure 4.2 hours @ $48	$201.60
	Scanning services: Anthem logo	15.00
	Courier delivery, 9/29/95	12.00
	TOTAL DUE	$228.60

TERMS: NET 15 DAYS

Thank you.

ing delayed sending your invoice, you can complete the job, include all the time and services on one invoice, and send it to the client. I feel free to vary my invoicing routine according to the client and the circumstances. With certain clients, I want to be very sure no work leaves my office until I have received payment; with others, I feel fully confident that an invoice mailed to the individual or company will be paid.

In some circumstances you may feel it desirable to collect a deposit when you begin working on a project. I have collected a 50 percent deposit from all resume clients for several years and find this practice reduces the number of "no shows"—people who never come back to pick up their resume. Having made a significant investment, they are more likely to want the completed work, even if they have gotten a job in the meantime. I have seldom requested a deposit from businesspeople; normally I do so only when I have some question about the solvency of the company or know from past experience that a particular client is a collection problem. (In fact, with clients whom I've had to chase to collect money due, I request full payment up front before doing any additional work.)

Rather than allowing a stack of unrecorded invoices to become a major chore at month-end, develop the habit of immediately entering information from each invoice into your bookkeeping system.

MANAGING CLIENT FILES

When a job is finished, you may wish to store a hard copy in your client file. In addition, always keep complete files on your computer system—including documents you have given to clients on disk at their request. I find it preferable to keep only the latest version of a document, unless the client specifically requests that I retain the older version intact when making updates. Filing clients' documents alphabetically on your hard drive is a logical method.

There are numerous options for storing your clients' computer files. Initially, you will no doubt keep everything on the computer's hard drive. This is faster and more efficient than trying to work off a disk. I'm also assuming that you will be backing up your hard drive *regularly and consistently*. How frequently you do this is up to you. You may not mind re-creating a week's worth of work in the event of a crash; or you may feel that daily backup is a better choice. The key is establishing a system so this task gets done regularly. My own system is backed up weekly—every Thursday night. You may want to run a backup every evening before shutting down for the night, or the last thing on Friday afternoon, or every other day first thing in the morning. This chore does not take very long to complete, since the backup software scans your hard drive and backs up only those files that are new or have changed. You can back up your hard drive onto a tape system (the least expensive method but not very accessible in the event you need to replace lost or damaged files); a Syquest or Bernoulli large-capacity system; magneto-optical drives with large-volume diskettes; newer large-capacity systems such as the Zip or EZ drive; or traditional 1.4-megabyte diskettes (their small capacity can make backing up the system a chore).

In addition to hard-disk backup, you should establish a system for periodically removing client files from your hard disk. As it becomes full, it will work less efficiently—also, your backup procedure will take longer and require more disks or tapes. The above-mentioned backup devices can also be used for supplementary storage, or you may want to consider a second hard drive. With large-capacity hard drives having become so reasonably priced, this is a cost-effective way to store client files that are not quite current yet not ready for true "dead" storage. When this drive becomes full, it may be possible to discard some no-longer-needed files.

Once you have copied the documents into storage, remove them from your active hard disk to free up space for future projects.

Disk backup and file storage are two good examples of necessary but nonbillable business activities—those things that go into the estimated 25 percent of your time that is not billed.

FINANCIAL RECORD KEEPING

One of your top priorities upon opening your business should be setting up a bookkeeping system that allows you to easily track and review a number of important financial facts and figures. Whether manual or computerized, your system should allow the following:

- Tracking of each individual profit center and expense category—to determine, for instance, what percentage of your business comes from graphic design, or how profitable your photocopier is based on a comparison of its costs and income.

- Sales-tax figuring, recording, and summarizing.

- Review of billings for individual clients.

- Selection of unpaid accounts for follow-up activity. (To make things really easy, try to combine your system with an automatic reminder to follow up on all accounts outstanding after their due dates.)

- Integration of your various methods of paying bills (checks, credit cards, finance agreements, cash) into your expense summary.

- The ability to compare income and expenses for various time periods—to track, for instance, how your income for the first six months of 1996 compares to the same period in 1995.

- Separate designations for capital equipment (an asset to the company that may need to be depreciated for tax purposes) and regular business expenses.

- Summary and detail reporting of all activities for your use in preparing monthly reports, comparisons, and year-end figures for tax returns.

While this information can be recorded and tracked manually, your computer is an ideal tool for these tasks. Financial-management software is inexpensive and usually easy to understand. Quicken, QuickBooks, and QuickBooks Pro (specifically designed for businesses that track time and prepare estimates) are three popular programs made by industry-leader Intuit Corporation. Financial-management software does a good job of transforming sometimes difficult, time-intensive activities into simple tasks that are actually fun to perform. (Try setting up a chart sometime showing your income growth since you started your business!)

Create an account for each income category you wish to track, or perhaps use one umbrella account with subcategories: "Additional Services" might contain such subcategories as faxing, photocopying, and scanning; "Outside Services" might contain printing, service bureau, and graphic design. Your main income category of desktop publishing may be broken down as well, if you wish; you might want to record design, type formatting, and data entry separately, if you will be offering services in all these areas, and particularly if you are charging different hourly rates for these services.

Expense categories should be listed as well. Again, consider using comprehensive accounts with subcategories—"Office Expenses" might include paper and office supplies, computer supplies, and miscellaneous office-related services; "Auto Expenses" might reflect costs for maintenance and repairs, gas, insurance, and fees or taxes.

The goal is to create a system that, with little effort on your part, makes it easy to review and assess your various sources of income and expense. For maximum usefulness, make your main categories conform to those used in the Schedule C tax return; that way, summarizing the totals in each category will give you the necessary information for tax-return preparation. If you plan to use an accountant for tax-return preparation, enlist his or her assistance in setting up your accounts. Accountant's fees spent at the beginning should pay you back in lower tax-preparation fees resulting from your expert organization.

To avoid making a chore out of your business bookkeeping, develop the habit of entering items immediately as they occur or, at a minimum, once a day. After entering expenses, immediately file receipts, credit card bills, checking account statements, and other financial documents that are relevant to your business. (You should keep a hard copy of these papers in the event of a tax audit.) In your income account you will need a system for tracking whether items have been paid so you can follow up as necessary. My system is to enter billed items when creating the invoice, then update the record when payment is received by recording payment date and check number, if appropriate, then stamping the back of the check for deposit.

Having a self-inking stamp of your business name and checking account number is a great convenience, saving you the time and effort of writing this information on the back of every check you deposit. By the way, you should be aware that checks made out to your business name must be deposited to your business account and cannot be cashed.

MANAGING YOUR CASH FLOW

When I think of the term "cash flow," I envision a beautiful stream of money on a smooth, steady journey toward me. Of course, there are times when the flow slows down to a trickle. If this happens to you more than occasionally, you should examine your business to determine if your volume of work is insufficient (in which case you may need to increase your marketing efforts) or if other factors are affecting the flow. Once you've pinpointed the problem, you can begin to address it. Let's examine a few common reasons for a slow cash flow—assuming your rates are high enough and your volume of work is steady.

Are you billing promptly? Or are you delaying this chore because of the press of deadline work that always needs to be completed? Perhaps you're not using your Project Tracker efficiently and find it difficult to prepare bills for large or complex projects. If that's the case, redesign the form or restructure your tracking system so that you keep current on time spent and services performed for each job. Then make it a point to invoice your client the minute you have completed a job. Most companies track due dates for payment of bills by the date they receive the invoice, not the date you performed the work.

Are large projects shutting off your cash flow? Perhaps you should be billing in interim stages for large ongoing projects. Sometimes a project is extended or, for varying reasons, goes on far longer than initially envisioned. If lack of cash flow is affecting your business operations, you should discuss with the client the fact that you need to bill for work performed to date. This is entirely reasonable, and in fact clients may prefer it because it allows them to track expenditures for the project and not be surprised by a large invoice at the end.

Are accounts uncollected after thirty days? This is probably the biggest reason for cash-flow difficulties. If you're counting on being paid within a certain time frame and the client doesn't comply, you could be in difficult straits. There's no reason to feel uncomfortable calling to collect payment for work you have performed, but for some reason this is a difficult task for many of us. There's no way around it but to bite the bullet and get it done. When preparing your monthly billing, compile a list of overdue accounts. Begin by placing a phone call to your contact at the organization and proceed, if necessary, to the Accounts Payable department. Your first call is a polite inquiry as to whether everything is in order, as you haven't yet received payment. Often this is enough to generate payment. Get a specific date as to when you can expect payment, and on that date call again if you haven't received it. In many cases it's merely administrative oversight or chronic disorganization that causes late payments. Be polite but persistent. Always make records of your conversations and attempts to collect, noting the time, date, person you spoke with, and results of your call (e.g., "check promised to be cut on the 13th," "now says check will arrive by end of week," etc.). This will be valuable documentation should you ever need to pursue the matter further. While you may feel hesitant to pursue money due for fear of causing a bad relationship with the client, keep in mind that you simply can't afford to work for someone who won't pay you. You will also want to be wary about extending credit to individuals or organizations once you've had trouble collecting from them. Requiring payment up front is entirely reasonable if it is based on a past history of difficult collections.

Is all your income billed at month-end? If you follow a policy of billing all your clients at the end of the month, you may find yourself with a very uneven cash flow. If this is the case, consider developing two or even three regular billing dates throughout the month—say the 15th and the 30th, or the 10th, 20th, and 30th. You will still bill clients once a month, on their date, but spreading out the billing dates means your income will also be spread out more evenly throughout the month.

Have you depleted your cash reserves? Perhaps you paid cash for new equipment, or paid a large advertising bill up front to achieve a significant discount. If this is a temporary situation, things should resolve themselves rapidly. But if you find you're constantly cash-poor and are having trouble paying your subcontractors, vendors, and suppliers promptly, then you need to examine your own bill-paying habits. Request credit accounts with suppliers so you can get the supplies you need today and pay for them in thirty days. Credit cards can be used to pay for many business expenses. (Designating one of your credit cards solely for business use makes it easier to keep track of your expenditures.) Just be careful not to overextend yourself with credit, and make it a priority to pay bills in full each month unless you charged a large-ticket item that you'd prefer to pay off over three or four months. Don't jeopardize the financial reputation of your business by letting your accounts payable become overdue.

Are you being sufficiently cautious about extending credit? You're not required to allow all your clients to have a credit account with you, and if you do allow this privilege, you are entirely justified in performing a credit check on the company. Ask your client or the company's Accounts

Payable representative for the names, phone numbers and fax numbers of three or four businesses from which they purchase services. Make a phone call or send a fax to each referral, asking about the client's payment history and how long they've been doing business with this supplier. If the answers are less than reassuring, you're perfectly justified in refusing to extend credit—this is a sound business decision. For many clients, it will be most advantageous for you to request payment at the time they pick up the completed work. Making this one of your policies ("unless alternative billing arrangements have been made in advance") leaves no chance for misunderstanding. With a client whom you suspect of being less than reliable, you can politely but firmly reiterate your policy of not allowing work to leave the office until it's been paid for. While you don't want to anger or alienate clients, remember that you must get paid for your work in order to stay in business.

For businesses with a lot of individual or small-business clients as opposed to larger businesses and corporations, it may be advantageous to accept credit cards for payment of invoices. With a credit card you are assured of getting the money, provided you have obtained the necessary authorization. You can acquire credit-card acceptance capability ("merchant status") through your bank or a third-party service (such as Discover/Novus; see the Appendix for contact information).

Keeping your financial house in order is an essential business task that you can make less burdensome with regular review, analysis, maintenance, and follow-up. Doing so will also help you keep on top of crucial obligations such as quarterly tax payments that, if neglected, can spell financial ruin for your business.

DEALING WITH COMPUTER PROBLEMS

Since your computer and peripheral equipment are crucial to your business operations, you should have in place a number of methods for getting help with conflicts, glitches, crashes, and other computer problems before they actually occur. Here are a few suggestions:

- *Dealer.* Your computer dealer is frequently your first line of defense, particularly if your equipment is still under warranty. Should you experience less-than-expert computer service, you might be able to locate other dealers that will also honor your warranty.

- *Service contract.* An on-site service contract is a wonderful convenience and, depending on the nature of the problem and your available backup equipment, may even allow you to keep working when a piece of equipment breaks down. For instance, if your laser printer needs repair, taking it in for service will require a certain amount of time and effort. Waiting in your office for on-site repair means you can continue to create documents, even if you can't print them. You will, of course, pay a higher price for on-site service, so compare what's available in your area before making a final decision. Some service owners choose not to purchase service contracts of any kind, preferring to pay for repairs as they are needed. This is a gamble that may pay off, particularly with normally very reliable equipment such as fax machines. My experience has been that service contracts for computers and printers have become considerably less expensive, while contracts for copy machines continue to be high. It will be your decision as to whether you want to pay for the protection a service contract affords.

- *Independent computer repair.* Numerous independent computer repair specialists have sprung up to support the tremendous growth of PCs in all areas of the country. Often these individuals provide great customer service and are extremely knowledgeable about repairing many kinds of office equipment. They may be willing to provide over-the-phone troubleshooting when a problem occurs and frequently provide on-site repair and maintenance services.

- *Manufacturer assistance.* Most computer and software manufacturers staff troubleshooting support services which can be accessed by phone (sometimes toll-free). When you can get through to them, the advisors are usually very knowledgeable and helpful. Long waiting times are typical, though, and frequently you have to go through the voice-mail runaround, which takes time and costs money each time you call.

- *Hotlines/helplines/networking.* Some organizations offer phone assistance by office staff or volunteer experts. This is a great source of free, knowledgeable help. Computer users' groups (such as the Boston Computer Society) and professional organizations (such as the National Association of Desktop Publishers and the National

Association of Secretarial Services) are among those that offer this service to members. You also may locate a knowledgeable individual or two among networking groups in which you participate. An additional source of technical help is some mail-order companies' toll-free lines—for instance, MacConnection/PC Connection provides excellent technical assistance. (See the Appendix for contact information.)

SCHEDULING APPOINTMENTS

Whether you choose to keep regular hours, during which you are open for drop-in visits by clients, or work by appointment only is a matter of personal preference. For most small, home-based businesses, seeing clients only by scheduled appointment is preferable. An appointment-only policy protects your clients' confidentiality, since they know there will be no other visitors in the office during their scheduled time, and it gives you the flexibility to schedule your work hours to suit your convenience. Also, not being available to drop-in visitors allows you to handle personal or work-related emergencies that inevitably crop up and may require you to leave your office unexpectedly.

If you work other than a traditional 9:00-to-5:00 schedule, rather than asking clients when they would like to meet, suggest specific times when you will be available—"I have an opening at 8:00 A.M. on Tuesday," or "I'm free at 6:00 on Thursday evening—does that fit your schedule?" These available times may very well include early mornings, evenings, or weekends—this is a definite advantage to a home-based business, and it is a convenience for both you and your clients. Clients don't need to know the details of your work- or home-life schedule, nor is there any reason to offer an excuse for not being available—a simple "I'm sorry, my schedule is full at that time" is sufficient.

Clients will need to visit you to drop off work and to pick up completed projects. These appointments are typically fairly short—reserving a half hour on your calendar will generally suffice for the client to discuss the project requirements with you briefly, or review and pay for completed work. More lengthy client appointments will occur from time to time for several reasons. During a client's first visit, you will want to allow time for at least a brief discussion of all the services you provide. Additionally, taking a few moments to get to know a new client will help to establish a friendly relationship. Often, too, new clients are unsure of your ability to grasp the complexities of their project and may spend the time to go over every detail, while more seasoned clients will feel perfectly comfortable leaving a folder in your drop box with their scribbled project instructions. Longer-than-usual client visits are also the norm when more than one individual is visiting—group discussion and decision making typically take longer than individual. And if a client is reviewing a complex project, or perhaps waiting while you make revisions, you can expect to spend additional time.

In cultivating client relationships it is essential to walk a fine line between being too brisk and businesslike and spending valuable time in idle chitchat. In a home-based business this can be particularly difficult. Often clients are friendlier and develop closer relationships when they visit a businessperson in his or her home setting. And if you are feeling isolated from being alone all day, you may find it easy and enjoyable to extend client visits by chatting, asking them about their families, discussing your golf game, and the like. This problem tends to resolve itself naturally. As you become increasingly busy, you will find it's just not possible to do this and maintain a high rate of productivity. Most likely you will jealously guard the work time you do have available since it may very well be erratic or frequently interrupted. It's important to be friendly with clients, of course, and you will no doubt enjoy the relationships you develop with many of them. But it's also good to become skilled at moving the conversation along and bringing it to an end without offending your clients.

Billing for Client Visits

Time spent discussing the requirements of your client's project is billable time. For most desktop publishing professionals, however, a typical five- or ten-minute initial review is not billed. The clock starts only when the client wishes to spend additional time to review the project in more depth, discuss various design possibilities, or ask for your recommendations. This consulting time may be delineated on your invoices, although I generally prefer merely to bundle the time in "desktop publishing and design services." Similarly, when billing clients you should include an additional ten or twenty minutes for client review and minor revisions. If more time than that is spent during the client review session, it generally reflects additional services requested by the client and therefore involves an additional cost.

On other occasions you may meet with clients at their offices. If the client specifically requests the meeting to discuss a project ("Why don't you come in and meet with our human resources people to talk about their ideas for the brochure?"), then it should be considered "design/consulting services" and billed appropriately. Sales calls and introductory visits, even if they result in work from the client, are generally not billed.

You will find you can rely on common sense in deciding whether to charge a client. Giving an excellent client ten or twenty minutes of "free" time is well worth it; doing the same for a sporadic client who has a history of making last-minute changes will only encourage this behavior. With my best clients, I frequently find the time, information, and advice I give them leads to additional work, and I almost never charge for this time.

CONVERTING INQUIRIES TO SALES

Waiting for the phone to ring at your new business can be a nerve-wracking experience, one that you can make less stressful by being fully prepared—well organized with systems in place to handle whatever challenge comes your way.

Professional Telephone Communications

There is little that turns off a prospective client more than speaking with a person unfamiliar with a business's products, services, and capabilities. To prepare yourself to respond confidently to phone inquiries, have ready your complete price list as well as an outline of typical projects and their associated costs (see chapter 7 for more information). Know your policies and procedures. Complete preliminary discussions with vendors for services you don't provide directly.

I'd also like to pass along some words of wisdom I learned from my dad, many years ago: "If you act like you know what you're doing, you'll never be questioned." Dad used this strategy often, with aplomb and to great effect—most memorably, when calmly and purposefully leading wife, eight children, and assorted friends or relatives to large tables in previously unopened restaurant sections. The restaurants in question were probably very wise in not insisting that we move—a large family group, all of whom are energetic conversationalists not shy about raising their voices to be heard, *should* be isolated as much as possible from other restaurant patrons! But the theory works very well in business life, too. If you authoritatively lead clients where you want them to go, for the most part they will be happy to submit to your expertise and put themselves in your (seemingly) capable hands.

If you exude confidence, this will be communicated to callers. People like to do business with experts; if you project your expertise, you will persuade your callers of it. This attitude will be very beneficial in converting those callers to clients.

Your business telephone should be answered on the first or second ring, if possible. Always state your business name. I usually greet callers with a friendly and positive "good morning" or "good afternoon." Smile before you pick up the phone—your voice will carry the smile through to the caller.

You may get callers who ask, simply, what your rates are. Instead of merely stating your hourly rate, try to obtain some additional information from the caller. The more you know about their needs, the more accurately you can provide price and other information to them. The request for information should be presented in such a way that they see it as a benefit to them: "I'd be happy to tell you my hourly rate, but it may be more relevant if I give you an estimate for your specific project. Can you tell me about it?"; or, "Certainly. Are you inquiring about desktop publishing or graphic design services?"

For marketing purposes, the more time you spend talking with a prospect about the proposed work, the better your chances for actually getting the job. An in-depth discussion allows you to convey your expertise and professionalism to the caller. Ask pertinent questions about their particular project to demonstrate that you know what is involved.

Some callers will wish to find out general information about your services and may not have a particular project in mind. In that case, draw them out about their business in general and ways they may have used desktop publishing firms in the past. Then pose a question that shows you understand different ways they might use your services.

Consistently answering the phone during business hours will permit you to capture the best response from your advertising. Frequently, callers looking for a specific service will compile a list of businesses—here again, you gain an advantage from being at the top of the list alphabetically. If your phone is picked up by an answering machine, many first-time callers will simply go on to the next name on their list without leaving a message. If you answer the phone promptly and professionally, provide relevant information, demonstrate that you are an expert at what they want done, and convey your confidence in your abilities, chances are good that the prospect will decide to bring the work to you without making further calls.

In reality, though, it's just not possible to answer the phone at all times during traditional business hours. If you have young children at home, answering the phone with their voices (and maybe screams or cries) clearly audible in the background will hurt your business more than it helps, at least with new clients. You are bound to be out of your office sometimes, whether running errands, meeting with clients, or just having lunch. If you have children at home with you for major portions of the day, using a portable phone to escape (to a closet or bathroom, if necessary) when the phone rings may work well for you. Some parents are successful at training their children to be quiet when the phone rings. I have found, in my case, that being on pins and needles, wondering how long the silence will last, is detrimental to the poised, confident image I am trying to convey!

When you cannot answer your phone, an answering machine or voice-mail system will do it for you. Having a system with a screening feature is very helpful—as you gain regular clients, you may not mind speaking with them when office noises are less than businesslike, as they will most likely be aware of your home/office setup. If new callers do leave a message, you can make an effort to return their call very promptly—before they have the chance to work very far down their list of businesses.

Scheduling productive work time can be a real challenge for a one-person, home-based business, and if you find that frequent phone calls interrupt the flow of your creative work, by all means turn on your machine and don't answer the phone. It's far better to have clients leave a message than for you to answer the phone when you are distracted, working madly against deadline, or not able to concentrate on the call. Try to avoid being rushed or harried when you pick up the phone. This attitude, too, will come across to callers. Leaving a message may be preferable to your clients, as well, since often there's no real need for them to speak with you. Just be sure to return phone calls or otherwise act on messages promptly and consistently so callers can be assured their messages are being received.

As you gain experience in dealing with phone inquiries, you will develop a sixth sense about when to push to close the sale and when to back off. In some instances it's effective and appropriate to ask, "When would you like to come in?" or, "Would you like to schedule an appointment?" Such a question would, of course, follow an exchange of information, and the caller would give some indication of being ready to proceed—even a long pause or hesitation may be the signal for you to pose the question. You then proceed to schedule the appointment and give directions to your location. Be sure to obtain the caller's telephone number so that you can be in touch in the event you need to reschedule, and close by reiterating the appointment time: "I'll look forward to meeting you, then, at 10:00 on Tuesday."

With other callers, you can sense that they're not ready to commit. I find it more beneficial to express my willingness to speak with them again when they have additional questions or have further refined their needs. It will not be to your benefit to prolong a phone conversation with a person in the very early stages of inquiring about desktop publishing services. You have gathered some information about their needs in general; end by offering to send some follow-up information about your business. This does several things: It puts you in control of the phone conversation and allows you to keep it fairly brief; it ensures that you obtain their name and address to add to your prospect database; and it allows you another opportunity to sell your services, when they receive your package of materials. It's a simple matter to compose a brief letter responding to their individual circumstances and demonstrating how you can meet their needs. Send the letter along with your brochure and business card. Chances are they'll call you again when they're ready to move forward.

EFFECTIVE CLIENT PRESENTATIONS

In some instances, you will gain work strictly as a result of a telephone conversation. In others, you may be asked to meet with prospects to discuss their project in more detail. When this occurs, in nearly every case you will have been prescreened, and the prospect will feel confident that you can do the job—they will certainly not wish to spend the time meeting and discussing their work with every desktop publisher in town. You may be the only one proceeding to the meeting stage, or you may be in competition with a few other services. But once you have been asked to meet with a prospect, you can proceed with confidence, knowing that you have passed the initial screening stage.

Meeting with clients in their offices is one occasion when you will definitely want to present your most professional, businesslike image—this usually means wearing a suit and carrying a briefcase or portfolio. If the business is in other than a corporate business environment (perhaps a retailer or a home-based consultant), it is still important to convey your best business appearance—perhaps a skirt or slacks and a jacket would be appropriate. It's far better to overdress than underdress for the occasion. Wearing a suit, even if others at the meeting are in casual shirts and slacks, indicates respect for their business and a serious attitude about your own.

Prepare yourself for the meeting by filling your portfolio with examples of your work that are pertinent to the client's needs or that demonstrate unusual and creative applications. Consider writing a brief summary of your understanding of the client's needs at this point and how you can meet them. Bring enough copies for everyone at the meeting (and a few extras), along with your brochures and business cards. If more than a few days elapse between the date the appointment is scheduled and the appointment itself, call the day before to confirm. Arrive for the appointment five minutes early!

During the meeting, spend a lot of time listening. Be respectful and interested in what they have to tell you. Ask clarifying questions. Take notes about specific requirements. When it's your turn to speak, be confident about your ability to do the job. If there are service requirements that you don't provide, tell the prospect how you will accomplish these—the vendors you'll use and your experiences with them in the past. This indicates that you understand the complexities of the job and aren't afraid to get outside assistance to ensure the work is done correctly. Show the samples in your portfolio, particularly those that are related to the client's job at hand. Summarize the procedures, deadlines, and desired outcome. Restate your expertise and experience. Be sure to express *enthusiasm*! Let the client know that you would *love* to do this job. This alone can be a strong selling point. (I've learned from several clients that the reason they awarded their business to me was because of my excitement and enthusiasm for their particular project.) Finally, pause. Take a breather. Look around at the various people at the meeting. See if there are any questions or hesitations. If you see none, by all means ask for the sale: "When can we get started?"

If questions do arise, consider them further opportunities for you to make the sale. Clients are looking for someone to solve a particular problem—the specific project they have in mind. Each time you overcome an objection by giving an expert answer, you are coming closer to being their problem solver.

On occasion you may hear objections that relate to whether it's *really* necessary to hire a professional desktop publisher for the job—after all, they have feature-filled word processing programs or even desktop publishing programs and could save a lot of money by doing it themselves. This type of objection can be minimized if, through your discussions, you have demonstrated a thorough grasp of the complexities of the project; conveyed your ability to handle all the details; discussed how you will be using vendor services, if appropriate; and demonstrated your expertise by showing your portfolio. When describing the projects within the portfolio, be sure to provide an explanation of what went into the job. It's likely that the clients don't have a real understanding of many of the processes involved in desktop publishing. The artistic effect you achieved from combining and editing a photograph with textured backgrounds may *look* simple, but in fact it was a complex process that required expertise in a number of DTP tasks—scanning, manipulating photos, combining art form styles, applying and adjusting color, and so on. By commenting on the process when displaying your samples, you further demonstrate your expertise and, at the same time, make it evident how much is really involved in good desktop publishing work. The process of educating your clients and prospects will contribute toward their appreciation of your skills.

Perhaps the client has a valid reservation about assigning this project to you, since it's somewhat outside your area of expertise. With some good clients you may be able to suggest that you "give it a try," but with other clients or prospects it may be more beneficial for you to refuse the project or suggest another resource if it is truly beyond your capabilities. Remember, your main objective is customer satisfaction, and you will not be able to fulfill the requirements of every desktop publishing–related job. It's far better to help the client locate a suitable service than to risk your client relationship and your reputation by producing substandard work.

You will likely be asked during a client meeting to give a cost estimate for the project. *Never* give on-the-spot exact quotes! In some cases, however, you can give an estimate—now that you have a full understanding of the project parameters, you know approximately how many hours it will take you to complete. When doing on-the-fly figuring like this, always bid high. Add at least 15 percent to your first guess before stating a figure to the client. And give a range rather than a specific figure. You might say something like, "Based on our discussion today and my understanding of the project requirements, the cost to write and design your festival flyer should be in the $300–$400 range." If the prospect blanches and says that they were only counting on spending $200, don't despair. You now know what their budget is and can tailor a proposal to fit that figure—naturally, you will have to scale down your services, but it's quite possible that a win-win solution can be achieved.

With complex projects it's difficult to factor in all the requirements on the spot. Resist the temptation to give even a ballpark estimate at this point. Most clients will fix that price in their minds, and when you come in with a more detailed (and undoubtedly higher) estimate after you've had a chance to give the whole project some consideration, the client may be dismayed. Instead, tell clients that you will put together an estimate and fax or mail it to them later that day—stress that you want to be sure it's accurate and need to study the requirements a bit, as well as consult with various subcontractors. Your completed estimate then becomes the reason for your follow-up call or visit—at which time you can ask the "when can we begin" question, if you weren't able to do so at the initial meeting.

PREPARING PROPOSALS AND ESTIMATES

As a follow-up to client meetings, or sometimes in response to phone calls, you will need to prepare proposals and estimates for clients' consideration.

In writing your proposal, follow similar procedures to those discussed above in the "client presentation" section. Summarize the job requirements and give an indication of how you will fulfill them—either by doing the work yourself or using outside vendors. (If the latter is the case, discuss the qualifications of the vendors.) Specify the "deliverable" for the project—exactly what it is you will be providing to the client. Next, provide a detailed cost estimate covering all aspects of the project, and outline your payment terms. Frequently a three-tiered payment plan is specified: one-third upon beginning work, one-third at some stated completion point (for instance, upon delivery of the completed first draft), and one-third upon delivery of the final version. Restate your qualifications and expertise. It might be appropriate to mention other similar projects you have done or attach samples of your work. Close by expressing enthusiasm for the project, and state that you look forward to beginning work.

In some instances you may wish to obtain the client's signature on the document, signifying acceptance of the price, authorization to begin work, and application of the first payment.

When preparing a job estimate, make detailed notes to yourself about your process of arriving at the estimate—you may need this later to back up your estimate when speaking with the client. Outline the entire job process so that you will be able to evaluate thoroughly the services and costs involved. Calculate the time the project is likely to take. If estimating a large project seems overwhelming, review two or three typical pages and estimate the time requirement for them; then factor this estimate into a total for the whole project.

(You will find it extremely helpful to establish "standards" for time and pricing parameters for a number of typical projects. These guidelines will assist you in giving quick price quotes for small projects and estimating larger ones. Chapter 7 contains information on some "classic" desktop publishing projects and guidelines for establishing your own standards using a Job Element Checklist.)

If you will be expected to meet with the client on an ongoing basis to discuss aspects of the job, be sure to include this time in your estimate. Time for meeting and discussing the project with vendors should also be included, along with the specific costs for these services. Include costs for courier or other delivery methods. Fixed costs (such as courier and sub-contractor fees) may be marked up your standard percentage or merely passed along. Be sure to allow in your estimate the time it will take for you to serve as a liaison with these vendors.

When you have completed estimating the project requirements, review the whole procedure to make sure nothing was left out. It's always a good idea to increase your time estimates by 10 to 15 percent to provide some breathing room. Then, insert your assumptions and cost estimates into the proposal.

As a general practice, I keep all estimates together in one folder until and unless they become actual jobs. Also included in this folder are copies of faxes or my own notes in response to client calls for a quick estimate. Sometimes quite a bit of time elapses between the request for an estimate and the awarding of the job, and keeping this documentation in one place enables me to put my hands on it quickly to review the initially specified job parameters and compare them with the actual requirements.

A good policy to establish in all your estimating procedures is to set the price slightly higher than you figure it to be and allow more time than you think you'll need. You'll then develop a reputation for coming in ahead of schedule and under budget. If, instead, you aim for the lowest possible bid and set unrealistic deadlines, the client is bound to be disappointed when you can't deliver.

April 19, 1995

Maryann S. Edmonds
Vice President, Marketing
Maple Valley Elder Services, Inc.
2900 Second Avenue, Suite 15
Maple Valley, OH 45000

Dear Maryann:

I enjoyed meeting with you and Nancy and learning about the requirements for preparing your operations manual. I was impressed with the professional, attractive look of Maple Valley's printed materials. As you know from my prior work for Pine Health Care, I have experience developing this type of manual, and it will be my pleasure to work with you on this project.

I have reviewed my notes from our meeting and propose the following project scope and specifications, timetable and fee:

PROJECT SCOPE AND SPECIFICATIONS

- Eight manual sections comprising approximately 240 pages, as much as 60% forms and the rest primarily text.
- Material prepared in PageMaker 5.0 / Macintosh.
- Design services will be provided for text, tables, and forms, and a template of all styles will be provided to you.
- Services to include review for editorial consistency. Minor edits to be made directly to material; significant discrepancies, inconsistencies or lack of clarity to be flagged for your attention.
- Corporate logo and graphics (supplied by you on disk) will be utilized as I feel appropriate to enhance the material. Additional graphics may be requested by me for preparation by your graphic designer.
- A good portion of the text material will be provided to me on disk.
- One revision following proofreading is included.
- Two laser-printed originals and one disk copy of all materials will be provided.
- Up to three visits by me to your facility for materials pick-up and drop-off and/or planning and review meetings are included, as are up to four courier deliveries for additional pick-up and/or drop-off.

PROJECT TIMETABLE

- Operations manual to be completed by June 3, assuming steady flow of materials to me to allow sufficient time to meet this deadline, and expeditious return of first-draft material following proofreading.

- Interim deadlines may be established and mutually agreed upon in order to facilitate proof-reading and review by Maple Valley staff.

PROJECT FEE

- For all services and materials as outlined above $4,540.00

- Payment terms and conditions: initial retainer of one-third ($1,500) to initiate services; second payment of one-third ($1,500) upon delivery of completed materials (first run-through); final payment of $1,540 upon delivery of revised masters. For the final two payments, invoices will accompany delivery of the materials; terms net 10 days.

- Additional services as mutually agreed upon will be invoiced upon delivery; terms net 10 days.

Should mutually agreed-upon additions to the above scope occur, or should the size of the document significantly exceed the 240 estimated pages, additional fees will be charged following discussion and mutual agreement. As well, should the size of the project be substantially less than estimated, a proportionately lower fee will be charged.

I look forward to beginning work on this project.

Sincerely,

Louise Kursmark
BEST IMPRESSION

CHAPTER SEVEN

WORKING WITH DESKTOP PUBLISHING

In work the greatest satisfaction lies—the satisfaction of stretching yourself, using your abilities and making them expand . . .
— **KENNETH ALLSOP**

This book is not a manual on how to do desktop publishing; rather, it addresses operating a desktop publishing business—and that's a whole different ballgame. Still, there is a fundamental knowledge base that is required to provide professional desktop publishing services. Many of the readers of this book are true DTP experts already, but this chapter is designed for those of you who are more at the beginning stages. Perhaps you have a background in word processing or office services, or you might be a skilled graphic designer with little knowledge of typography. Guidelines and good practices for producing professional DTP documents will be discussed. We'll also look at some classic desktop publishing projects in more detail and examine a job process from start to finish.

CREATING DISTINCTIVE DOCUMENTS

Two effects of the computer revolution are vitally important to you as an independent desktop publisher:

1) It is possible to do nearly *anything* with words and pictures on a page using widely available, reasonably affordable software and hardware. This capability gives you unlimited creative opportunities.

2) With this wide availability, many of your clients and prospects have their own personal computers. They come to you because of your expertise and creativity in creating professional documents.

It's important that you strive to make your work stand out from the crowd of laser-printed pages flooding the business world. This can be done through good design, an eagle eye for detail and accuracy, correct typography, and creative use of graphics.

One of the easiest ways to create a distinctive document is to give it a different look from all the other pages being produced by computer users everywhere. Installed with every word processing and desktop publishing program are specific default settings with regard to font, type size, line spacing, margins, etc. The majority of users continue to create documents with these defaults, primarily because they see no reason to change them—and probably don't know how, anyway. I make it a practice *never* to produce a page that conforms to the typical defaults: one-inch margins all around, Times 12 point/automatic line spacing, ½-inch paragraph indents, double spaces between paragraphs. (More about each of these specifications below.)

Another important element to creating a professional desktop-published document is the correct use of typography. Learning to *typeset* rather than *type* is essential. Leaf through a few books on your shelf—you'll see that they don't look like typed pages. The technology has been created to mimic book publishing, not typewriting, so it's important to learn to use it properly.

The guidelines that follow will help you avoid the "default" look, escape common errors found in word processed and desktop-published documents, and improve the professional quality of your work.

TYPOGRAPHY AND STYLE GUIDELINES

Vary your fonts. In particular, avoid the two most widely used fonts, Times and Helvetica. There's nothing inherently wrong with either font—they're both extremely useful. The main reason for avoiding them is *because* they are so widely used. There are thousands of fonts available. You'll need several good text fonts (serif and sans serif), including some that look good at very small point sizes; a few heavy, bold headline fonts; and some special-effect fonts and scripts for use as appropriate. Adding to your font collection from time to time is fun and can inspire your creativity in new directions. When purchasing text fonts, look for a complete family—the font should be available in a number of variations such as italic, bold, bold italic, heavy, condensed, and the bold and italic versions of heavy and condensed. Having all these elements will ensure you can use compatible fonts in all parts of your publication. "Multiple master" fonts, available from Adobe, allow nearly infinite variations while keeping the font pure and in conformance with its original design. Headline and special-effect fonts normally come in only one or two variations.

The two widely available kinds of fonts are PostScript and TrueType. It's a good idea to use only PostScript or only TrueType fonts and not mix the two in one document. If you do, you're risking font conflicts and slow printing. Also, be aware that most service bureaus use PostScript fonts. Check with several service bureaus in your area to see if any of them can accommodate TrueType fonts.

Vary leading (the space between lines of text in a paragraph). The default line spacing present in most programs is, in my opinion, too close for text and too widely spaced for headlines. Allowing more space between lines in your paragraphs makes them easier to read and more attractive, while in a headline, closing up the space gives a better effect. You may have used a word processor or typewriter that allowed space-and-a-half or double spacing, but this is not typically available in desktop publishing programs. Instead, play with the line spacing or leading command so you get exactly the look you want.

Check for accurate line spacing. Inaccurate line spacing is an extremely common error in documents of all types. If your line spacing is set at "auto" or "default," increasing the size of one character (such as an initial cap) will cause the line spacing within the paragraph to be affected. Sometimes this occurs when an invisible element—such as a space or a paragraph return—is set at a different size.

Use paragraph spacing. Specifying space before and/or after a paragraph is much more effective and controllable than using two returns to space down to the next paragraph; it looks more professional, too. And it ensures you won't have blank lines at the top of a column when text flows onto the next page.

Set your own tabs. Don't be lazy. The ½-inch tab settings that are the default on most programs are simply not correct for many documents—most obviously, in most cases a ½-inch indent for the first line of a paragraph is just too big. Learn the use of left, right, center, and decimal tabs. Use the program's tabs features to position the text where *you* want it.

Adjust margins. There's nothing sacred about an inch on every side. Learn the edge restriction of your individual printer—it may be a ½ inch, ¼ inch, or less. With flyers, brochures, and strong graphic pieces, it is usually more effective to go closer to the edge of a page, while with text-heavy documents it will enhance readability and appearance if you bring the margins in.

Don't underline. This is a holdover from typewriter days, when the only ways to make words stand out were to use <u>underlining</u> or ALL CAPS. Computer-generated underlines are almost always too close to the text and are unattractive. Instead, choose italics, bold, or both to indicate emphasis. Use your design to make words stand out—large fonts, different fonts, reverses, initial caps, and other techniques.

Don't underline—but do *use rules* for design and emphasis. Rules are lines running below and/or above a paragraph, usually the full width of the text column—though desktop publishing gives you control over the placement, size, and design of rules. Rules are available in word processing programs, too—learn 'em and use 'em!

Don't use all caps. Words set in all caps are more difficult to read. Also, using all caps often requires major kerning (individually adjusting the spacing between letters). As noted in the underlining paragraph, experiment with different ways to make your words stand out. (And if you use all caps online, you'll be accused of SHOUTING all the time!)

One space after a period (and all punctuation). Yes, I know it's hard to break this habit. But if I can do it, so can you. With typing, two spaces were necessary for that pause after a sentence. With typesetting, the punctuation, spacing, and letter forms make that extra space unnecessary. Using two spaces frequently causes unsightly gaps in a block of text—particularly if it's justified.

No double dashes! Learn when "em" and "en" dashes are called for, and how to create them on your computer system, and then use them. Traditional usage is not to put spaces on either side of the em dash. Lots of people prefer the spaces, though—just be consistent throughout the document.

Use curly quotes. With the Macintosh, it's been possible for years to set the curly or "smart" quotes as a default (although you can also create them at any time using the option-bracket and option-shift-bracket key combinations). On the IBM, newer versions of word processing and page-layout software offer this option as well. If yours doesn't, find the correct key combination to create them.

Use the right punctuation. Learn or brush up on the use of semicolons; always put periods inside quotation marks; be careful with parentheses; master the use of the apostrophe; use the computer ellipsis instead of three periods; and so on.

Watch your spelling. Use the program's spell-check feature one last time before going to final output. Have a good dictionary so you can look up words that the spell checker doesn't know. Be particularly careful with names and places—these are not in most spell checkers' dictionaries.

Use the right word—even if your client uses the wrong one. Should it be *counselor* or *councilor*? *adverse* or *averse*? *principal* or *principle*? Your bookshelf should include at least one of the many available books that specialize in answering just these kinds of questions. Clients will be very grateful for this kind of editing (just be sure you're right).

Proofread obsessively. A good routine is to use the spell-checker; do a light on-screen proofing; print out the first draft; with red pen in hand, read the draft and mark corrections and design changes; make the corrections; print out again; read twice, once for spelling/grammar/proofreading errors, once for sense; make any corrections; run spell-checker again; print out final; proofread once through. (This process assumes a mainly text document and will be extended if you are reviewing and revising your design throughout this process.) Sure, it's a lot of work—but for a professional desktop publisher, what's more important than a perfect page?

Use copyfitting techniques so that there are no awkward line endings, widows, or orphans (paragraphs that end with one or two short words or go on to the next page with just one line). Copyfitting is the practice of rewriting copy to improve a document's appearance and adjust its length to fit in the available space. How much rewriting you can do depends on your agreement with your client. Even if you don't have the authority to change a word, you should make necessary formatting adjustments to improve the document's appearance.

Use styles. All good word processing and desktop publishing software allows the user to create and utilize specific styles—font and size, leading, attributes such as bold or italic, space before or after the paragraph, indents, tabs, and other settings. Recent versions of some popular programs now allow you to set styles for individual characters as well as an entire paragraph—for instance, you can create one style for newsletter body copy and an additional character style for a first paragraph drop cap, then apply them instantly with just a click or two of the mouse or a simple keyboard combination. One of the wonderful benefits to using styles is that you can change the style description and—voila!—the text itself will automatically change to match the new style. This is particularly helpful when you wish to present two or three design possibilities to a client. Change styles, page setup, and graphic elements, and in just a few minutes you have a totally different-looking document. Mastering your program's style function will make your work easier and more consistent. From my experience of training novices and experts alike in both word processing and desktop publishing programs, this is the one feature that most often draws the "Wow! Why didn't I learn that sooner?!" response. So do yourself a favor and learn that feature *now*—you'll find yourself using it daily.

Remember that rules are meant to be broken. Of course, for a variety of reasons, you may choose not to follow all these rules all the time. The main excuse for "incorrect" usage is an extremely important one—that could very well be the way your client wants it. But being knowledgeable about the generally acceptable standards for typography will allow you to make informed choices.

DESIGN GUIDELINES

How do you define good design? What makes a printed page effective? Why is one DTP design better than another?

The answers to these questions are subjective—it's likely each person reading this book will have different answers. The important thing to remember is that you are a *commercial* designer. Your work must convey your clients' messages and meet their objectives. No matter how original, artistic, creative, or beautiful the document you design, it is worthless unless it is also *effective*. So keep that in mind as you apply your creative and artistic skills for your clients' benefit:

For a flyer or poster—Is all the information there (who, what, when, where, why)? Is it easy to read? Does it grab the attention of passers-by? Does it convey the image of the event or activity?

For a brochure—Is the company's image appropriately portrayed? Is the text readable, or are there too many long paragraphs of densely packed type? Is it well organized? Is it easy for readers to respond?

For a newsletter—Does the design add to the message? Is the style in keeping with the material (businesslike, playful, serious, fun, etc.)? Is it readable? Are the most important stories most prominently placed? Do the graphics complement the stories, or are they merely decorative?

Each printed piece has a purpose; it's your job as a designer to contribute to that purpose. Don't let the design overshadow the content.

As you become more skilled at desktop publishing and are exposed to a variety of printed documents, you will come across things that "work" from a design standpoint. You will find yourself focusing in on the design details of every document you see, wondering how a particular type effect was created, critiquing the piece for its effectiveness, and generally improving your overall eye for design. Start keeping a file of samples you particularly like or dislike to spark your own creativity when you are starting a project. Carla Culp (CLCulp & Associates, Edwardsville, Illinois) calls this her "snitch file." Many desktop publishers keep one. Naturally you would not copy a design directly, but reviewing others' work can give you good ideas to adapt for your own.

ACCEPTING AND PROVIDING DISKS

It's very likely that clients will wish to give you data on disk for your use in designing and formatting their documents. In theory, this is a great idea. It allows the client to work with the text extensively before formatting is applied, thus reducing the likelihood of major text changes further along in the design process. It may save you hours of keyboarding time and free you up to do the design and layout—functions that are usually more enjoyable and more highly paid. Problems can arise, however, when clients don't have a good understanding of how text is utilized in a DTP document. When drafting their document, clients may be concerned about how the material looks on their screen—which may not conform with the way it will look when you're done with it. The purpose of providing material on disk (to save your time and the client's money) will be defeated if you have to do extensive cleaning up of the material—removing duplicate tabs, paragraph returns, spaces, all caps, and the like. To make this transfer more successful, it may be helpful for you to create some guidelines for clients who wish to supply material on disk. A sample guideline sheet is on the following page.

Virus-protection software is an essential tool to use each and every time you pop a "foreign" floppy disk into your computer—i.e., a disk, even one of your own, that has been anywhere else. The best virus programs provide frequent updates to guard against newly created viruses and also have the capability to remove a virus once it's detected.

It's also quite likely that from time to time clients will ask you to give them their documents on disk. This may present a dilemma to the desktop publisher: Should you hand over the disk, giving up control and possibly eliminating a need for the client to use your services in the future? Or do you refuse to give it up, causing hard feelings? And how much work should you do to ensure that clients can actually use the disk you give them? These are decisions you should think about ahead of time so that when the time comes, you're prepared to respond. Let me share my feelings on this subject and the procedures I've followed.

One of the most crucial issues is "ownership" of the material. Do you, the designer, own it? Or does the client, who paid for it? The concept that the work belongs to the creator is more frequently held by designers/artists or possibly traditional typesetters. In fact, it was quite

professional desktop
publishing services

9847 Catalpa Woods Court
Cincinnati, Ohio 45242

513-792-0030

GUIDELINES FOR PREPARING
DISK FILES FOR OUR USE

We glady accept text files on disk. Since the purpose of providing these files is for you to save money by saving us time, please be sure to prepare files with a style and format that we can use easily. Often client disk files require more work to undo formatting than would be required to re-enter the text. To avoid this problem, simply consult the following guidelines.

FILE FORMATS

We can accept most word processing formats, Mac or IBM. If we can't read your file, you can probably save it in another format that we can read, or we can get it converted. Our preferred format is Microsoft Word 5.1/Macintosh.

We can accept 3.5-inch diskettes easily. If you have only 5.25-inch floppies, let us know and we can probably get them converted.

Include a printout of what's on the disk. You can mark this copy with instructions regarding layout and design or even text edits you'd like us to complete. Please mark clearly and legibly, in red ink if possible.

Keep a backup copy of what you're sending us—just in case . . .

Provide a listing of files on the disk, if there are more than a few. Be sure to clarify any file names that may not be readily apparent to us. Delete any unnecessary files from the disk.

TYPE FORMATTING GUIDELINES

Don't apply unnecessary formatting to your document. Chances are we'll have to undo it. You can, however, apply formatting such as bold, italics, etc., to individual words at any time—this formatting is usually retained.

Don't use underlining or all caps. These are "typewriter holdovers" and are seldom used in desktop publishing. It's also much more time consuming for us to undo this formatting than it would be to apply it in specific instances where it is desired.

When using tabs, hit the tab button only once. You don't need to bother with setting up tabs in your program, and don't worry about how the page looks on your screen. Your efforts to make the setup look right (especially if you rely on default tab settings) will involve extra work for us. We can easily set the appropriate tabs.

Single space between paragraphs. Double space only between major sections of the document.

Don't hit the return key until you reach the end of a paragraph, even if you're intending to wrap text (for example, for indented bulleted lists). We'll set it up so the text wraps automatically.

Keep it simple. Straight text with minimal formatting is easy for us to work with, and providing it on disk will indeed save you money.

Call us if you have any questions!

common some years ago for an "ownership" policy to be a formal policy of the firm. One rationale for such a policy is that if you lose control of the work, others quite possibly could make changes that will reflect badly on your expertise and decrease the value of your work. And since your name may be identified with the document as its initial creator, you may have a strong interest in protecting its integrity. Additionally, particularly with regard to original artwork, you may feel entitled to a royalty each time the art is used for commercial purposes. If your position is that you retain ownership of the work, be sure to make this a formal policy and be clear about it with the client when you first begin working together.

My feeling has always been that the client pays for the work, and therefore the client retains ownership of it. I always give my clients work on disk when they request it. I charge a reasonable fee for this service (typically $5 for simple disk copying, more if I need to adjust the file or do a file conversion). I'd rather clients keep coming back to me because they want to, not because they're chained to me by the documents I alone can access. Additionally, it's been my experience that unless the client is a skilled desktop publisher and has access to comparable software, equipment, fonts, and graphics, he or she will have difficulty working with that file to create a document of the same quality. In a way, giving clients their material on disk reinforces the professional quality of the work I do for them. As well, I believe it's in my best interest to maintain a cordial relationship with my clients. Refusing to give up a disk may ensure that I keep a particular job within my own business but will not contribute to the possibility of my doing additional work for the client—it will merely label me "hard to work with." So, when requested I always provide this service, willingly and cheerfully. I also keep my own copy of the material, in the event the client corrupts the file in some way and then wants to have me work on it again.

The following incident, which occurred fairly early in my desktop publishing career, crystallized my philosophy on providing client work on disk. A neighbor of mine who owns a manufacturing company was having his price list—six pages full of tiny type, part numbers, and prices—typeset and printed at a printer's in a rather out-of-the-way location. As we became friendly and he learned about my business, he decided it would be very convenient to have me make the text revisions to the price list. He planned on continuing to have it printed in the same place as he felt some loyalty to that printer, having worked with them for several years. I instructed him to ask for the price list on disk and told him that in all likelihood I would be able to work with the existing file (it was a PageMaker document). When he did so, he was first informed that the price list was the printer's property and could not be released. My neighbor persisted, and after quite a bit of effort he came to my office in triumph, bearing a disk. You can imagine our dismay and stupefaction when I opened the disk to find that the printer had saved the file as an EPS (encapsulated postscript) file—thus making it exist only as a graphic, not as editable text! In other words, we could print out the price list as it was but could not make changes. Extremely annoyed by this tactic, my neighbor elected to sever his relationship with the printing company, and I re-created the entire price list from scratch. What did the printer gain by refusing to supply the file? As you can see from this real-life example, he gained nothing and lost a loyal, long-time customer. It's quite possible he had a policy of retaining ownership of files, but this was not made clear to my neighbor. Think about what you can gain and lose by supplying or not supplying client work on disk; then formulate a policy and be up front about it with your clients.

While I willingly make disk copies for clients, this is not to say that I guarantee clients can in fact use the files I provide. Unless requested to do so at the outset, I don't make a conscious effort to make my files compatible with my clients' computer capabilities. I do the job for them using the best tools I have available. If at a later time they request the disk, I warn them that there may be font or other file incompatibilities—they may not even own the software I used to create the document. If they then request that I make changes to meet their computer capabilities, I can certainly try (at my usual hourly rate), but doing so will very likely alter the appearance of the document significantly—most DTP files cannot simply be converted to word processing, for instance. I also make this clear to them and indicate that if in the future they want me to design a document with their capabilities in mind, I can certainly do so as long as we set up these requirements at the beginning.

DETERMINING THE PRICE OF A JOB

You've established an hourly rate and fee structure for your business—but are you still stumped when it comes time to provide an estimate or bill a client for work performed? It can be particularly difficult when you're asked on the spot how much something will cost. While it's reasonable to tell clients you'll study the project requirements and get back to them with a quote if it's a long or complex assignment, for relatively simple or recurring projects, you should be able to review the job requirements and quickly come up with a figure. It's usually best to give a range rather than a precise quote. You might say it will cost "around $200" or "between $80 and $120," for instance. Clients understand that your numbers are not precise, but they will expect the finished job to be billed in the vicinity of your initial estimate. (So be sure to discuss with your client as soon as they become evident any unusual problems or unforeseen difficulties that may affect the final cost.)

To establish your price for a project, it's necessary to consider all the elements that go into it. Some of these can easily be forgotten when you're quickly reviewing a client's requirements. Consider using a checklist of job elements and, from that checklist, developing a price list of appropriate ranges for common desktop publishing jobs. As you gain experience, you'll become comfortable with what a job "should" cost and quickly be able to factor in additional requirements to provide a close ballpark estimate.

You might even feel comfortable going over your checklist with clients. This will give them a good idea of exactly what goes into a particular project and may include items they hadn't even considered. If your price then comes in higher than expected, clients will understand why. Using the checklist will also help you frame questions to clients as to what exactly is required.

Following is a suggested Job Element Checklist, along with filled-in examples for several typical desktop publishing projects and sample design projects relating to the hypothetical projects.

The first example outlines a fairly typical brochure project. Imagine that you meet with an occasional client, ABC Corp., to discuss preparing a brochure for them. Since you have worked together before, the meeting is fairly brief—you already have a good understanding of the company's

JOB ELEMENT CHECKLIST/ESTIMATING WORKSHEET

Job _____

Client _____

SERVICE	HRS	RATE	OTHER/NOTES	TOTAL
Initial meeting with client				
Prepare estimate				
Additional consultation/research/discussion				
Subcontractor liaison				
Prepare text (input)				
Prepare text (write/edit)				
Prepare artwork				
Preliminary design/layout (# versions to be provided:_____)				
Proofread/revise/finalize first draft				
Client review/discussion				
Draft revisions/corrections/fine tuning				
Client review/discussion				
Final revisions/corrections/fine tuning				
Final client approval				
Prepare output: laser				
Prepare file for output: imagesetter				
Discuss/deliver file to service bureau				
Check output/deliver to printer/review specs				
Check/deliver to client/discuss				
Billing/filing/disk storage				
OTHER				
TOTALS				

Estimated Project Total _____

Provided to _____ Date_____

JOB ELEMENT CHECKLIST/ESTIMATING WORKSHEET

Job _____ Brochure _____

Client _____ ABC Corp. — Jim Logan _____

SERVICE	HRS	RATE	OTHER/NOTES	TOTAL
Initial meeting with client	.6	$50		$30
Prepare estimate	.2	$50	Incl. printing	$10
Additional consultation/research/discussion				
Subcontractor liaison	.3	$50	Discuss/get est.	$15
Prepare text (input)	.3	$20		$6
Prepare text (write/edit)				
Prepare artwork			Scan logo	$10
Preliminary design/layout (# versions to be provided: 2-3)	1.6	$50		$80
Proofread/revise/finalize first draft	.4	$50		$20
Client review/discussion	.3	$50		$15
Draft revisions/corrections/fine tuning	.4	$50		$20
Client review/discussion	.2	$50		$10
Final revisions/corrections/finalize first draft	.3	$50		$15
Final client approval	.2	$50		$10
Prepare output: laser	.1	$50		$5
Prepare file for output: imagesetter				
Discuss/deliver file to service bureau				
Check output/deliver to printer/review specs	.3	$50		$15
Check/deliver to client/discuss	.2	$50		$10
Billing/filing/disk storage	.1	$50		$5
OTHER Subtotal				$256
			Courier	$15
			Printer	$195
TOTALS	5.6			$466

Estimated Project Total _____ $500.00 _____

Provided to _____ Jim Logan _____ Date _____ 11/15/95 _____

Take care of the future...

...support medical and nursing education

The Carter Medical Scholarship Fund

established in 1980

Educating for the future.

The Carter Medical Scholarship Fund

1275 Washington Street
Anytown, Ohio 45000
(513) 555-8080

administered by
The ABC Corporation
Cincinnati, Ohio

Donation Form

I would like to make a donation to: **The Carter Medical Scholarship Fund**

☐ General Donation in the amount of $ _____
☐ Memorial Contribution in the amount of $ _____

In memory of: _____
Acknowledgment to family of deceased to be sent to:
Name _____
Address _____

Contributor's Name _____
Address _____

Please return this form with your contribution to: John Finch, Secretary • 1275 Washington Street, Anytown, OH 45000
Checks payable to: Carter Medical Scholarship Fund

Taking care of the future...

Your tax-deductible contribution will help medical and nursing students from Greater Cincinnati with the cost of tuition, equipment and books.

Your gift, large or small, will allow the continued growth of the Carter Medical Scholarship Fund to help educate the doctors and nurses of tomorrow.

The Carter Medical Scholarship Fund was started in honor of Dr. and Mrs. Maynard Carter, parents of ABC Corporation founder Alan B. Carter. Dr. Carter served as a medic in World War II and came to know medics and other medical professionals who, he learned, would be unable to complete their medical education after the war due to family priorities or lack of funds. After establishing his medical practice in Cincinnati in 1948, Dr. Carter vowed to work toward the goal of assisting worthy medical students to achieve their goal of becoming doctors.

Dr. Carter's first office nurse, Alma Hunt, soon became his wife. Mrs. Carter also felt strongly about helping others. While studying nursing, she herself had to drop out of school to care for ailing parents. When returning to finish her studies, she could only attend school part time due to the need to hold a paying job to help support her family. Together over the years, Dr. and Mrs. Carter quietly gave financial assistance to numerous medical and nursing students, and they became highly regarded in the medical community for their generous support of medicine-related education.

The ABC Corporation, a medical supply company founded by Alan B. Carter in 1975, is proud to continue Mr. Carter's parents' work. The Fund, started with ABC Corporation seed money of $10,000 in 1980, today has assets of more than $250,000. Grant aid is derived solely from the interest on investments and the generous contributions of members of the community, and the ABC Corporation provides no-cost administration of the Fund.

The Carter Medical Scholarship Fund...

Provides financial grants to local residents attending medical and nursing school.

Evaluates qualified candidates based on academic standing, personal character, and financial need.

Represents a variety of medical and community interests through its board of fifteen trustees, who supervise administration of the Fund.

image and typical job requirements. During the meeting you establish the purpose of the brochure and the client's expectations. The client requests simple graphics, including the company logo, which you will scan. Text will be provided in handwritten or rough-typed format for you to input. You agree to supply two or three initial designs, and the client will then select one version for revisions. You agree to handle the printing for the brochure and include this cost in your estimate. The brochure will be printed in black ink with one spot color (specified by the client) on the company's usual paper stock. With this knowledge, you know that you'll only need to spend a brief amount of time discussing project requirements with the printer.

When preparing your estimate, you plan on two review/revision processes, knowing that this client typically is not difficult to work with, likes the work you have done for them in the past, and doesn't often make copy changes. You can therefore plan on minimal time for additional client discussion as the project progresses. You estimate a total of $256 for your services on this project, plus out-of-pocket costs for printing and courier delivery of the finished brochures to the client. You therefore propose a total project cost of $500 to the client.

Based on the example given, you might establish a brochure design and production standard of three to six hours, or $150 to $300 if your hourly rate is the $50 used in the example (not including out-of-pocket costs). The range can be accounted for by variations in time to meet with clients (probably higher for a new client), allow for client review and revisions, work with a service bureau or printer, and so forth.

The following sample documents and Job Element Checklists—for a newsletter, a client identity package (letterhead, envelope, business card), a menu, and a flyer—will give you an idea of what *might* be involved in each project. Using the Checklist will help to ensure that you don't inadvertently forget to allow time for an important project element and therefore shortchange yourself in the estimating process. (Refer to chapter 6 for additional information on preparing proposals and estimates and a sample Proposal Letter.)

It's important to note that all the standards you develop should include total time on the project, start to finish, including all billable client meeting times, liaison with vendors, pick-up and delivery, review and revisions, and final production. Using the Job Element Checklist ensures that all these elements are included in the total cost you project to your client. As noted in chapter 6, be sure to specify the number of review cycles included in the project. On occasion a project may go through additional revisions as a result of changes made by the client. If this is the case, and if you have specified the standard, you can appropriately charge an additional fee for the time required to make the client's alterations. In my experience, including two to three reviews by the client is reasonable; anything beyond that is usually due to significant changes requested by the client or reflects a client who needs to tinker with a project continually.

Consider preparing the Job Element Checklist in your spreadsheet program so that dollar amounts are automatically calculated as soon as you enter the appropriate time increments. This will greatly speed up the process of preparing estimates.

Newsletter. With a newsletter, it is important to consider initial design and preparation time for the first issue and typical production time for each issue. You may choose to spread the initial cost over each issue, perhaps increasing your price by $50 to ensure that you recoup that amount within a year's time (using the numbers given in the example). I generally prefer to bill the first issue at a higher price and subsequent issues at the standard price. This ensures I'll get paid for my initial time even if the company decides to discontinue the newsletter and also presents a more accurate per-issue cost to the client.

Based on this example, you might develop a standard for newsletter production after the initial issue to reflect a per-page time requirement of 1.2 to 1.5 hours. Using our hypothetical $55 hourly rate, the client's cost would be $66 to $82.50 per page. (Developing a per-page standard makes it easier to come up with a total issue cost for any size newsletter.) Some newsletters include repeating elements—production or attendance lists, welcome to new members, employee anniversaries, and the like. If it is predicted that some pages of the newsletter will retain a standard format from issue to issue, your time to insert the new information would be significantly lower than that for laying out new pages, so you should reflect this in your estimate. Also, if each issue requires extensive graphic design or original artwork, your time estimates would need to be increased.

Corporate Identity. In this example, your client asks you to design a corporate identity package for his new building maintenance company. In

JOB ELEMENT CHECKLIST/ESTIMATING WORKSHEET

Job _Newsletter: quarterly, 8-page; initial plus subsequent issues_

Client _Mullins Real Estate — Patricia Mullins_

SERVICE	HRS	RATE	OTHER/NOTES	TOTAL
Initial meeting with client _Review content each issue._	1.0	$55		$55
Prepare estimate				
Additional consultation/research/discussion	1.0	$55		$55
Subcontractor liaison				
Prepare text (input)			On disk/my specs	
Prepare text (write/edit)				
Prepare artwork			Inc. w/ design time	
Preliminary design/layout (# versions to be provided: _1_)	3.6	$55		$198
Proofread/revise/finalize first draft	1.0	$55		$55
Client review/discussion	.4	$55		$22
Draft revisions/corrections/fine tuning	.6	$55		$33
Client review/discussion	.4	$55		$22
Final revisions/corrections/fine tuning	.4	$55		$22
Final client approval	.2	$55		$11
Prepare output: laser	.3	$55		$17
Prepare file for output: imagesetter				
Discuss/deliver file to service bureau				
Check output/deliver to printer/review specs	.6	$55	Color seps	$33
Check/deliver to client/discuss	.4	$55		$22
Billing/filing/disk storage	.2	$55		$11
OTHER _Total for each issue_	10.1			$556
Add for initial design:				
Client meeting/prepare estimate	1.5	$55		$83
Design template/review/revise	2.3	$55		$127
Add for first issue:				$210
TOTALS				

Estimated Project Total _$520-$600 per issue plus $220 initial issue_

Provided to _Pat Mullins_ Date _1/8/96_

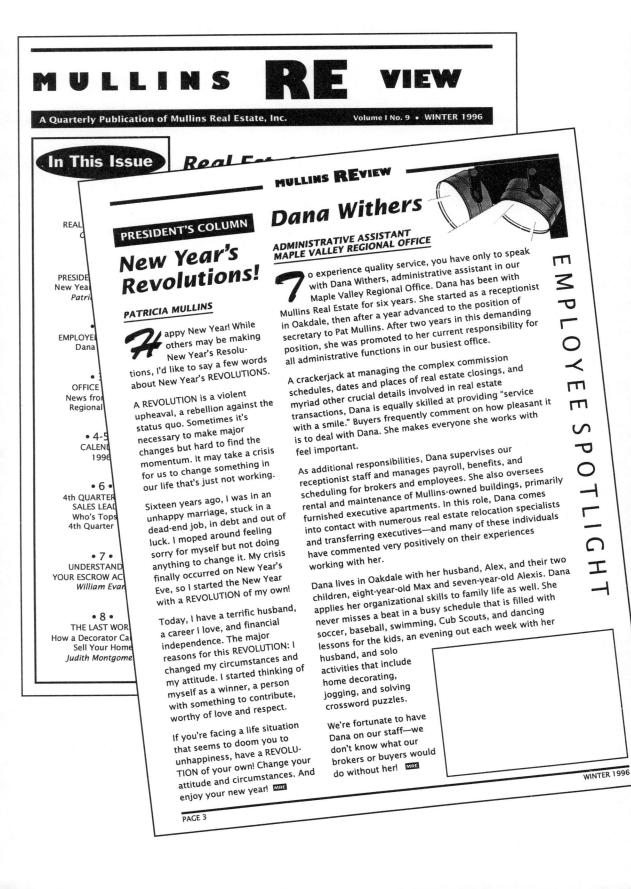

MULLINS RE VIEW

A Quarterly Publication of Mullins Real Estate, Inc. Volume I No. 9 • WINTER 1996

In This Issue

Real Est...

REAL ...
C...

PRESIDE...
New Yea...
Patri...

EMPLOYE...
Dana ...

• 3 •
OFFICE ...
News fro...
Regional...

• 4-5 •
CALEND...
1996...

• 6 •
4th QUARTER ...
SALES LEAD...
Who's Tops...
4th Quarter ...

• 7 •
UNDERSTAND...
YOUR ESCROW AC...
William Evan...

• 8 •
THE LAST WOR...
How a Decorator Ca...
Sell Your Home...
Judith Montgome...

MULLINS REVIEW

PRESIDENT'S COLUMN

New Year's Revolutions!

PATRICIA MULLINS

*H*appy New Year! While others may be making New Year's Resolutions, I'd like to say a few words about New Year's REVOLUTIONS.

A REVOLUTION is a violent upheaval, a rebellion against the status quo. Sometimes it's necessary to make major changes but hard to find the momentum. It may take a crisis for us to change something in our life that's just not working.

Sixteen years ago, I was in an unhappy marriage, stuck in a dead-end job, in debt and out of luck. I moped around feeling sorry for myself but not doing anything to change it. My crisis finally occurred on New Year's Eve, so I started the New Year with a REVOLUTION of my own!

Today, I have a terrific husband, a career I love, and financial independence. The major reasons for this REVOLUTION: I changed my circumstances and my attitude. I started thinking of myself as a winner, a person with something to contribute, worthy of love and respect.

If you're facing a life situation that seems to doom you to unhappiness, have a REVOLUTION of your own! Change your attitude and circumstances. And enjoy your new year! **MRE**

Dana Withers

ADMINISTRATIVE ASSISTANT
MAPLE VALLEY REGIONAL OFFICE

*T*o experience quality service, you have only to speak with Dana Withers, administrative assistant in our Maple Valley Regional Office. Dana has been with Mullins Real Estate for six years. She started as a receptionist in Oakdale, then after a year advanced to the position of secretary to Pat Mullins. After two years in this demanding position, she was promoted to her current responsibility for all administrative functions in our busiest office.

A crackerjack at managing the complex commission schedules, dates and places of real estate closings, and myriad other crucial details involved in real estate transactions, Dana is equally skilled at providing "service with a smile." Buyers frequently comment on how pleasant it is to deal with Dana. She makes everyone she works with feel important.

As additional responsibilities, Dana supervises our receptionist staff and manages payroll, benefits, and scheduling for brokers and employees. She also oversees rental and maintenance of Mullins-owned buildings, primarily furnished executive apartments. In this role, Dana comes into contact with numerous real estate relocation specialists and transferring executives—and many of these individuals have commented very positively on their experiences working with her.

Dana lives in Oakdale with her husband, Alex, and their two children, eight-year-old Max and seven-year-old Alexis. Dana applies her organizational skills to family life as well. She never misses a beat in a busy schedule that is filled with soccer, baseball, swimming, Cub Scouts, and dancing lessons for the kids, an evening out each week with her husband, and solo activities that include home decorating, jogging, and solving crossword puzzles.

We're fortunate to have Dana on our staff—we don't know what our brokers or buyers would do without her! **MRE**

EMPLOYEE SPOTLIGHT

your initial meeting, you sell your client on one of your services, a simple logo design for a flat fee of $75. You also agree to work with a printer on paper recommendations and present several to the client when he reviews the first draft. With this type of project, there is not usually a great deal of revision done to the design, so only two review cycles are included.

In preparing a standard for the design of letterhead, envelope, and business card, keep in mind that clients will request different levels of design services. Some wish merely to have their name, address, and other pertinent information placed attractively on the page, while others may wish you to spend time or use an outside service to prepare an original logo. Also, once you have developed the initial design, preparing companion pieces is normally very quick. Often I find it most efficient to present three or four letterhead designs to the client, then develop the additional pieces once the design has been approved.

Using the example, with a modest charge for design services and an hourly rate of $40, a range for an identity package might be quoted as $200 to $300, including paper recommendations and liaison with both service bureau and printer. For the client with simple design needs who will print directly from your laser output, a much lower standard could be established—perhaps $60 to $140.

Menu. This example illustrates a very simple DTP project: improving the appearance of an existing document, in this case a diner menu. "Before" and "After" examples are provided, to give you an idea of the appearance of typical client-created pages. You'll note that minimal client meeting and review times are included in the Checklist. Unless the client has a very specific vision to convey and wishes to spend time discussing it, there will be many projects where you will simply be asked to "make this look good." Projects of this size also involve no complicated billing or filing and typically are completed in two client visits (drop-off and review/pick-up).

More elaborate menus will, naturally, involve increased time for client meetings, design, and review, so these should be included in the Checklist and your estimate. Fine restaurants and country clubs can provide an excellent opportunity for creative, unique desktop designs.

Flyer. Many elements may be included in flyer production, such as writing or developing the necessary information, creating graphics, and arranging the page so that it is eye-catching and clearly presents the

JOB ELEMENT CHECKLIST/ESTIMATING WORKSHEET

Job ___Letterhead, envelope, business card___

Client ___Steve Livingston, Livingston & Associates___

SERVICE	HRS	RATE	OTHER/NOTES	TOTAL
Initial meeting with client	1.0	$40		$40
Prepare estimate *Given verbally during mtg.*				
Additional consultation/research/discussion				
Subcontractor liaison *Printer*	.5	$40		$20
Prepare text (input)				
Prepare text (write/edit)				
Prepare artwork *Logo design*				$75
Preliminary design/layout (# versions to be provided: _3_)	1.0	$40		$40
Proofread/revise/finalize first draft	.3	$40		$12
Client review/discussion	.3	$40		$12
Draft revisions/corrections/fine tuning				
Client review/discussion				
Final revisions/corrections/fine tuning	.3	$40		$12
Final client approval	.2	$40		$8
Prepare output: laser				
Prepare file for output: imagesetter *Color seps/film*	.2	$40		$8
Discuss/deliver file to service bureau *Modem*	.3	$40		$12
Check output/deliver to printer/review specs	.4	$40		$16
Check/deliver to client/discuss	.3	$40		$12
Billing/filing/disk storage	.2	$40		$8
OTHER *TOTAL MY SERVICES*				$275
Service bureau: film				$20
Printer				$205
TOTALS				$500

Estimated Project Total ___$275-$300 plus vendor services___

Provided to ___Steve Livingston___ Date___2/22/96___

LIVINGSTON
BUILDING
MAINTENANCE

75 N. Adams Street, Suite 6
Anytown, Massachusetts 01010

Tel. (617) 555-1234
Fax (617) 555-2345
Pager (617) 555-3456

Stephen T. Livingston PRESIDENT

LIVINGSTON
BUILDING
MAINTENANCE

75 N. Adams Street, Suite 6
Anytown, Massachusetts 01010

LIVINGSTON
BUILDING
MAINTENANCE

Tel. (617) 555-1234
Fax (617) 555-2345
Pager (617) 555-3456

75 N. Adams Street, Suite 6, Anytown, Massachusetts 01010

Stephen T. Livingston   PRESIDENT

JOB ELEMENT CHECKLIST/ESTIMATING WORKSHEET

Job ___ Menu

Client ___ Jerry McIntosh, Mighty Mac's Diner

SERVICE	HRS	RATE	OTHER/NOTES	TOTAL
Initial meeting with client	.2	$50		$10
Prepare estimate	Given verbally during mtg.			
Additional consultation/research/discussion				
Subcontractor liaison				
Prepare text (input)	.3	$24		$8
Prepare text (write/edit)				
Prepare artwork				
Preliminary design/layout (# versions to be provided: 1)	.6	$50		$30
Proofread/revise/finalize first draft	.2	$50		$10
Client review/discussion	.1	$50		$5
Draft revisions/corrections/fine tuning				
Client review/discussion				
Final revisions/corrections/fine tuning	.1	$50		$5
Final client approval				
Prepare output: laser				
Prepare file for output: imagesetter				
Discuss/deliver file to service bureau				
Check output/deliver to printer/review specs				
Check/deliver to client/discuss				
Billing/filing/disk storage				
OTHER				
TOTALS				$68

Estimated Project Total ___ $65-$75

Provided to ___ Jerry McIntosh ___ Date ___ 3/15/96

MIGHTY MAC'S FINE DINER

160 Main Street, North Anytown

555-4321

SANDWICHES

SUPER MIGHTY ROAST BEEF	$ 3.65
REGULAR MIGHTY ROAST BEEF	$ 2.70
JUNIOR MIGHTY ROAST BEEF	$ 1.95
PASTRAMI	$ 3.57
SLICED TURKEY	$ 3.05
HAMBURGER	$ 1.98
CHEESEBURGER	$ 2.13
DOUBLE HAMBURGER	$ 2.10
DOUBLE CHEESEBURGER	$ 2.40
HOT DOG	$ 1.35
FISH SANDWICH	$ 2.25
CHICKEN SANDWICH	$ 2.50

CHEESE WITH ANY SANDWICH   ADD $ .15

PRICES DO NOT INCLUDE SALES TAX

SIDE ORDERS

FRENCH FRIES	SM. $ .99	LG. $ 1.99
SPICY FRENCH FRIES		$ 2.25
ONION RINGS		$ 2.50
CHICKEN FINGERS		$ 4.75
MOZZARELLA STICKS		$ 3.99
PIZZA ROLL		$ 1.50
EGG ROLL		$ 1.50

BEVERAGES

COKE — DIET COKE —		SM. $ .89
SPRITE — ROOT BEER —		MED. $ .99
HI-C LEMONADE — FR. PUNCH		LG. $ 1.25
ICED TEA, COFFEE		$ 1.05
HOT COFFEE, TEA	SM. $ .65	LG. $ .85
MILK	SM. $ .65	LG. $ 1.05

HOURS

SUNDAY	5 P.M. - 12 A.M.
MONDAY	CLOSED
TUESDAY	CLOSED
WEDNESDAY	11 A.M. - 2 P.M. 6 P.M. - 12 A.M.
THURSDAY	11 A.M. - 2 P.M. 6 P.M. - 2 A.M.
FRIDAY	11 A.M. - 2 P.M. 5 P.M. - 3 A.M.
SATURDAY	11 A.M. - 3 A.M.

Mighty Mac's Fine Diner

160 Main Street ◆◆ North Anytown

555-4321

◆ Sandwiches ◆

Super Mighty Roast Beef	$ 3.65
Regular Mighty Roast Beef	$ 2.70
Junior Mighty Roast Beef	$ 1.95
Pastrami	$ 3.57
Sliced Turkey	$ 3.05
Hamburger	$ 1.98
Cheeseburger	$ 2.13
Double Hamburger	$ 2.10
Double Cheeseburger	$ 2.40
Hot Dog	$ 1.35
Fish Sandwich	$ 2.25
Chicken Sandwich	$ 2.50

◆ *Cheese with any sandwich*   add $ .15

◆ *Prices do not include Sales Tax*

◆ Side Orders ◆

French Fries	Sm. $ .99	Lg. $ 1.99
Spicy French Fries		$ 2.25
Onion Rings		$ 2.50
Chicken Fingers		$ 4.75
Mozzarella Sticks		$ 3.99
Pizza Roll		$ 1.50
Egg Roll		$ 1.50

◆ Beverages ◆

Coke — Diet Coke —	Sm. $ .89
Sprite — Root Beer —	Med. $ .99
Lemonade — Fruit Punch	Lg. $ 1.25
Iced Tea, Coffee	$ 1.05
Hot Coffee, Tea	Sm. $ .65 Lg. $ .85
Milk	Sm. $ .65 Lg. $ 1.05

◆ Hours ◆

Sunday	5 PM - MIDNIGHT	Thursday	11 AM - 2 PM / 6 PM - 2 AM
Monday	CLOSED	Friday	11 AM - 2 PM / 5 PM - 3 AM
Tuesday	CLOSED		
Wednesday	11 AM - 2 PM / 6 PM - MIDNIGHT	Saturday	11 AM - 3 AM

JOB ELEMENT CHECKLIST/ESTIMATING WORKSHEET

Job ___ Flyer — Holiday Showcase _____

Client ___ Frances Adams, Sycamore Village Garden Club _____

SERVICE	HRS	RATE	OTHER/NOTES	TOTAL
Initial meeting with client Garden Club board mtg.	1.0		No chg/Donation	
Prepare estimate Given verbally during mtg.				
Additional consultation/research/discussion				
Subcontractor liaison				
Prepare text (input)				
Prepare text (write/edit)	.5	$60		$30
Prepare artwork	.5	$60		$30
Preliminary design/layout (# versions to be provided: 1)	.8	$60		$48
Proofread/revise/finalize first draft	.2	$60		$12
Client review/discussion	.3	$60		$18
Draft revisions/corrections/fine tuning				
Client review/discussion				
Final revisions/corrections/fine tuning	.1	$60		$6
Final client approval				
Prepare output: laser				
Prepare file for output: imagesetter				
Discuss/deliver file to service bureau				
Check output/deliver to printer/review specs				
Check/deliver to client/discuss				
Billing/filing/disk storage				
OTHER				
TOTALS	3.4		2.4 billable	$144

Estimated Project Total ___ $150–$175 _____

Provided to ___ Frances Adams _____ Date ___ 10/30/95 ___

Sycamore Village Garden Club presents its 6th annual

HOLIDAY

★ ★ **Tour eight of Sycamore Village's historic homes dressed in their full holiday finery.**

★ ★ **Warm up with mulled cider, Christmas cookies, and other holiday treats at each stop.**

8 Hart Lane
17 Hart Lane
77 High Street
85 High Street
101 High Street
72 Church Street
320 Church Street
471 Market Street

★ ★ **SPECIAL ACTIVITIES**

★ **Victorian gift-wrapping**
8 Hart Lane

★ **Ornament painting**
77 High Street

★ **Wreaths and outdoor decorations**
85 High Street

★ **Decorative candles**
471 Market Street

All programs begin on the half-hour and run for 30 minutes. Materials fee of $10 per activity; no charge to observe.

SHOWHOUSE

December 1-2-3 ★ *8-9-10* ★ *15-16-17*
Friday 6-10 PM ★ *Saturday 3-7 PM* ★ *Sunday 1-4 PM*

Donation: $3/house ★ $20/8-house ticket
Proceeds benefit Sycamore Village Scholarship Fund

important data—dates, locations, costs, and so on. This hypothetical example involves creating a flyer for a benefit community event. Note the Job Element Checklist indicates a "donation" of the time to attend the club board meeting to learn the specifications for production of the flyer. Donated time should be indicated on the invoice so organization members are aware of the true value of the service provided. This job required writing and editing of text for the flyer and design of a major graphic element, the "showhouse" logo. Creating a flyer that does not require writing, editing, extensive client consultation, or graphic design services might require one to one and a half hours, or $60 to $90 at the $60 hourly rate used in this example.

DEVELOPING A PROCESS

Sometimes just getting started is the toughest part of a job, particularly if you are a relatively inexperienced desktop designer. It helps to structure the way you take your project from start to finish. While there can be as many such processes as there are desktop publishers, I've provided an outline of the process that I've developed over the years that works well for me for a large variety of projects.

- *Review/clarify parameters of job.* Verify format and job specifications. Remind myself of unusual or difficult parts of the job—not to forget the mailing panel on a brochure, for instance, or confirm that extensive text editing will be required for space purposes. If I'm working on a lengthy project such as a newsletter, I organize the various materials that I'm working with—photographs, advertisements, special inserts, and reminder notices, along with the standard articles, to give me a general idea of how crowded this particular issue will be.

- *Review/enter text.* If text is coming to me on a disk, I open the file and check to see if it needs any reformatting (and do it), then skim the text. If I'm entering the text, I do so in my word processing program, applying no formatting at this point. Having a general understanding of the content and tone of the piece helps me to create a design that complements the message. For a lengthy piece such as a newsletter, I prefer to create each article as a separate document; for a shorter project such as a brochure, I usually enter the text all at once, first one side of the brochure, followed directly by the other. A spell-check is run on all text, whether created by me or imported.

- *Formulate preliminary design.* While some designers prefer to sketch out a design with pencil and paper, my drawing skills are so poor that this is not an effective procedure for me. I review fonts, skim through books of clip art, and sometimes check my portfolio or sample file (of my own or others' work) for ideas. I establish a vision of what the finished piece will look like, based on my knowledge of the purpose of the piece, the client's budget, and the content I have just reviewed.

- *Create master page(s) and styles.* Next I go to my page-layout program and set up the document pages with the correct dimensions and margins. I usually set up master page elements at this point, although sometimes I will wait to see how the text looks when laid out. I also establish text styles for body copy, heads and subheads, indents, captions, and other text that will be needed, based on my preliminary font decisions. Using styles means that all these fonts can be changed easily if the design doesn't look good, needs to be more compact or more spacious, or doesn't create the effect I envisioned.

- *Import text.* Now I begin placing text into the document, applying styles to each text file as it is imported. (Some desktop publishers find it more efficient to apply styles while text is being entered in the word processing program.) I produce a very rough layout, with blank spaces for graphics or unknown elements and too-long text extended below the page. Once all the text is imported, I have a good idea of whether the font size and leading are appropriate. Sometimes, if I can see that I'm way off, I'll revise my styles at this point, changing size or leading or even the font itself.

- *Import graphics.* This step may involve editing clip art in my drawing program prior to importing it into PageMaker, scanning a company logo or other graphic, devising graphic elements for the master page or between paragraphs of text, and in general bringing into Page-Maker all the graphics I think I'll be needing. All the graphics are placed in approximate positions, again to give me an idea of size and the spaciousness of the piece.

- *Fine-tune the design.* Now that I have all the elements available, I spend time making everything fit properly and look good. Also at this time I create lines, boxes, forms, additional text, and other elements produced directly in PageMaker.

- *Look over each page and print first draft.*

- *Review and proofread.* Red pen in hand, I give the project a once-over for general appearance, flagging any elements that need improving or correcting, then proofread all text.

- *Refine.* Then it's back to the computer to fix mistakes and improve the design. On occasion I'll be very unhappy with the piece and completely redo fonts and graphics; at other times my first attempt is nearly perfect. For the most part, though, it's somewhere in the middle—small refinements and improvements.

- *Print, review, proofread.* Reviewing the second draft involves, first of all, casting a critical eye on each page to see how it looks—in effect, standing back from my work and trying to get the big picture. Then I compare the pages to my red-marked first draft to be sure I've incorporated all the changes and proofread the entire thing once again.

- *Revise.* The revisions are made, a final spell-check is run, and the final proof is printed out. At this time I also create additional versions of the piece if I plan to produce them for the client. Often I prepare two or three versions of a newsletter design, a brochure, letterhead, and the like for clients to review, using different fonts and graphics to convey different images.

- *Final review.* Revisions, review, and proofreading continue until I'm satisfied. Sometimes the third time is sufficient, and I'm ready to call the client to say that the project is complete; at other times I find it difficult to be completely satisfied. When this happens after numerous attempts, if possible I put the project aside for awhile and look at it with fresh eyes at a later time.

- *Clean up.* Once a project is complete, I record final time charges on the Project Tracker and, if appropriate, prepare a bill and enter the total into my bookkeeping system. I also discard my red-marked draft copies, put away clip art and font selectors, place the finished work and all client materials into the client folder, and tidy up my desk before starting the next project.

Naturally, some projects involve extra steps, such as discussions with a printer or graphic designer, paper selections, or calls to the client with questions or problems. The entire process may be completed in an hour or proceed over several days or weeks, and of course the job is not complete until it has been reviewed and proofread by the client and a final version approved and printed.

CHAPTER EIGHT

MANAGING YOUR BUSINESS AT HOME

Life is short . . . it's up to you to make it sweet.

— SADIE DELANY

n envisioning running a home-based business, you may wonder if you'll be able to summon the motivation to work when faced with the lures and distractions of having your home and family so nearby. In my own experience, and from conversations with dozens of other home-based entrepreneurs, just the opposite is true: We find ourselves short-changing other areas of our lives to make more time for our businesses. Our constant struggle is to find time to fulfill all of our roles: business owner and operator, parent, partner, homemaker, family organizer, individual. And, since the great majority of us are energetic, ambitious, efficient, and committed to our goals, we want to excel in all of these areas, and we want to do them all full time! Coming to grips with our own limitations is an essential but sometimes difficult exercise. We need to accept that we can't do it all and focus on the things that matter the most—the things in life that "make it sweet."

Each of us has unique priorities and circumstances. This chapter discusses numerous common dilemmas faced by home-business owners. As you read it, try to get a handle on those things that are most important to you, and find your own balance. An earlier chapter talked about "juggling skills"—here is where they come in especially handy!

MAKING TIME FOR YOURSELF

Little things, like regular haircuts and television, and big ones, like exercise and sleep, are always the first thing to go. While certain personal sacrifices may be necessary from time to time, it's a mistake never to take time out just for yourself. Scheduling self-care routines into your day or week will make an enormous difference to your overall well-being.

Sleep seems, for many busy home-business entrepreneurs, a colossal waste of time. If we only had those extra hours to use every day, just *think* what we could accomplish! But it's a mistake to cut down on your sleep too much. While under crisis conditions you may be able to function very well on only a few hours' sleep, eventually it will catch up with you. And if you're operating in crisis mode *all the time*, you'll find you have nothing in reserve. But you may discover you need less than the traditional eight hours of sleep—I've found that I can function perfectly well averaging six hours of sleep a night, and when necessary can go for a day or two on three or four hours. Experiment with your sleep times to see how an hour or so less sleep affects you over a few days or a week.

Establish an exercise routine that you enjoy and that fits your busy but flexible schedule. A noontime walk or bike ride, a 6:00 A.M. or 6:00 P.M. aerobics class, twenty minutes on the treadmill midmorning, thrice weekly visits to a nearby fitness club, your own dance routine with weights—whatever it might be, find it and do it. Regular exercise improves your overall health and definitely increases your energy level.

Leisure activities, either alone or with family or friends, should not be forgotten. And don't leave them to chance—schedule a weekend away, a lunch date, a visit to a bookstore, and put them on your calendar, so they become as important as your business appointments.

HOUSEKEEPING

When faced with an overstuffed life, many of us choose early on to accept less-stringent housekeeping standards. We each seem to find a certain level of neatness or messiness that is tolerable and that we can justify because of work and family priorities. Your own personal tolerance for less-than-perfect housekeeping is important to consider. I strongly recommend hiring a housecleaner as soon as you are busy enough to justify it. While a weekly or biweekly cleaning will not guarantee an always-orderly home, it will free you from essential cleaning chores and assure that your home is *clean* even if it's not always *neat*!

SEPARATING BUSINESS AND HOME LIVES

When your business is in the next room, it's sometimes difficult to "turn it off" at the end of a work day to focus on your family or other nonwork activities. The temptation is always there to spend a few extra minutes or hours on a job, to get a head start on your next day's work, or to begin an exciting creative project. Even worse is the tendency to be thinking about your business all the time, even when you're not physically in the office. This is a mental struggle many of us go through—separating ourselves from our businesses. Try to win this battle. Your friends and family will soon become irritated and annoyed if they find you can only talk about work or are distracted all the time. Practice shutting off your work mind when you leave your office.

Another problem that sometimes crops up is clients who take advantage of the fact that your business is home-based to drop by at unusual or unscheduled times in hopes of finding you at home. Worse still are clients who call you on your residence line if they can't reach you on the business line! It's up to you to take firm control of this situation before it becomes a problem.

Let's imagine you are faced with the situation of a client ringing your doorbell during dinnertime. You answer the bell, not knowing who it is. You are slightly surprised to see your client, who naturally does not have an appointment at this hour. Somewhat apologetically, she says, "Sorry I didn't call first—I just thought I'd stop by on my way home to discuss this project with you for a minute." You can, of course, say, "Sure! Come on in!" and spend the next twenty minutes talking business while your dinner cools and your family wonders what's happened to you. The problem with being accommodating to a client in this manner is that now you have set up the expectation that she can drop by at her convenience, without scheduling an appointment, any time she wishes. She will very likely do it again—and you really can't blame her, because you let her get away with it the first time. Instead, maintain control over your time and your business by responding in a friendly, professional manner, along these lines: "I'm sorry, but I'm not able to meet with you right now. I'd be happy to give you a call in the morning to talk about your project." It's also a good time to remind the client about your drop box, available for clients' convenience after hours. The occasional client may try to insist that it will "only take a minute or two to go over this." Again, be pleasant but firm in asserting your nonavailability. Assuming you provide ample opportunity for client meetings, it is not at all unreasonable to insist on not being disturbed by business at other times.

The same strategy should be applied with phone calls. If your home number is listed, it's readily available to clients—and some of them will take advantage of this situation. I've found it a good strategy to be nonconfrontational—to explain to the caller that I'd prefer they call on my business line to be certain I'm available to discuss business. With most callers, this statement suffices. If I'm actually in the office, I ask that they call on the business line "next time" and proceed with the discussion; if I'm not working, I ask that they call the business number and leave a message.

Of course, there will always be a few clients who think the rules don't apply to them. One evening I was preparing dinner when I heard my business phone ring. The answering machine responded, and a client left a message to call back. A few seconds later, my home phone rang. It was the same client, who said, "Oh, I hoped you might be home. You can ignore that message I just left you." He then launched right into a discussion of his work requirements. After overcoming my stupefaction, I was forced to interrupt him in midsentence, to tell him that the reason I didn't answer the business phone was because I was not working. He found it somewhat difficult to accept that my being home did not automatically mean I was working. This type of insensitivity is rare—just be sure to nip it in the bud if it does crop up.

Sometimes the question arises as to whether you should answer your business phone during nonbusiness hours. This is very much a matter of personal choice. When your business is new, it's difficult *not* to answer every call. Perhaps a major new client is on the other end of the line, or someone with a need for a rush project that you can certainly accommodate. The only problem with this approach, again, is that you build up an expectation that you are available practically "round the clock." While it may seem far from burdensome to treat a few clients with this type of accommodation, it's likely you'll grow to resent the intrusions as you become busier and need to set more limits on your work time. When that happens—when you find yourself getting annoyed at the clients who call at odd hours (quite possibly the very clients you were delighted to speak with a few short months ago)—then it's time to stop answering the phone except during business hours. If you are diligent about getting back to clients who leave messages on your answering machine, you will do a fine job of meeting clients' expectations. If there are a few long-time clients who will find this a significant change from the way you have normally done business together, then you should address the issue with them. Alert them to the fact that you most likely won't be answering the phone at midnight or 6:00 A.M. or whenever they were likely to call. Assure them that they can leave a message and you'll get back to them promptly. Without being at all apologetic or defensive—and certainly not letting them know that they annoy you when they call—try to word your notice in such a way that they see it as a benefit to them. You might say that you've restructured your work day and should be more available to speak with them during regular business hours.

In my experience, for the most part clients have been extremely respectful of my time and my schedule, and I will frequently go out of my way to accommodate them—but it's *my* choice if I decide to talk business during my nonwork hours.

BALANCING YOUR WORK AND HOME LIVES

You will soon be spending time with clients, and they are certainly important. But be sure to make time for the other essential people in your life: your family and friends.

Your Children

Although many home-based-business owners start their business with the stated intent of "spending more time with my children," it's quite easy to get caught up in business priorities, deadlines, and the lure of more-work-more-money.

Try to make a conscious effort to spend dedicated time with your children so that they'll feel as essential as your business. Reward them for playing quietly while you're working by letting them choose an activity and participating in it fully with them. Arrange "kid stops" while running business errands. A trip to the library, lunch out, or fifteen minutes at the playground can help you both enjoy the outing.

Teaching your children the value and pleasure of work is also a good and enjoyable lesson. You might pay them for performing small tasks around the office or allow them to do "paperwork" at your work table.

Every stage of childhood presents unique challenges to parents. With very young babies, it's their unpredictable schedules and immediate needs. Naptime and feeding routines change almost daily, making it hard to plan work time or schedule appointments. Toddlers are into every-thing and need to be watched at all times; preschoolers may talk constantly, need to be entertained, or start to develop social schedules that keep you running. Once children are in school you can count on some measure of predictability, but your ingenuity may be challenged during vacations and over the summer. A sense of humor, flexibility, and the ability to roll with the punches will help immeasurably as you try to meet your children's needs and manage your business.

For the past few years I've operated my business on a schedule that conforms roughly to my children's school hours. That has meant starting at a traditional time in the morning (somewhere between 8:00 and 9:00) and working steadily until early afternoon (2:00 or 3:00). Then comes a lengthy break during which I spend time with the children, run errands (many of them work-related), prepare and eat dinner, do the dishes, supervise homework and baths, read stories, tuck the babies in, and try to spend a few moments in adult conversation with my husband. Then it's work time again, typically from 8:00 until midnight or 1:00 A.M., with occasional evenings off for community activities, meetings, and the like. When things get *really* hectic, a few extra work hours can be squeezed into the day by getting up early and polishing off a project before breakfast.

My children frequently accompany me on errands, so I try to make it enjoyable for them and also limit my errands to their capacity. In the past they loved visiting the printer, where they were frequently given boxes filled with a delightful assortment of castoffs—paper, label, and cardboard scraps and samples. They also eagerly accompanied me on regular deliveries to one particular client who kept a candy jar on the counter!

As witness to the fact that there are more positives than negatives in having a parent who works at home, here is a brief essay written by my daughter several years ago.

MY MOM, THE BUSIEST PERSON IN MASSACHUSETTS

by Meredith Kursmark

My mom started her business right after I was born. She's been working at it for over ten years. Because she started it when I was born I can't imagine what it would be like if she worked away from home. There are things I like about her job and things I don't.

Some things I like are:

- She works at home so she can drive me places.
- She has two computers, two printers, and two copy machines that I can use for school projects. I also use the computer for computer games.
- She has some really nice customers.
- She has her own hours, which means she can take time off if she wants to, for going to the movies and coaching my team in softball.
- She knows tons about computers so she can help me if I'm stuck.
- She has lots of colored paper and art supplies that I can use.
- I can put labels on envelopes or stuff them and get money for it.

There are only a few things I don't like about her working at home. They are:

- She is almost never on time to pick me up from school or other places.
- She is very busy and has to work on weekends.

Child-care Options

Having always had young children while running my business, I've experimented with a wide array of child-care options. Although it's possible to keep your children at home with you all the time, I don't recommend it. It's my opinion that either your work or your children—or both—will suffer if you try to give both of them your attention at the same time. It seems much more sensible to have a reliable child-care provider for at least part-time coverage. During the hours your child is in day care, you can devote full attention to your business, arrange client meetings, and be extremely productive. Other dedicated work hours can be fit in during your children's sleep times, whether early in the morning, at night, or during the day, and projects requiring low concentration can be performed while the children are up and about. My best child-care arrangement occurred when I was fortunate enough to find a qualified, dedicated, nurturing home-care provider who required a full-time commitment. Knowing that I had the option of having my son cared for anytime from 6:00 A.M. to 6:00 P.M., Monday through Friday, gave me enormous flexibility. He spent only about four or five hours a day with her, on average, but I was able to extend his hours when necessary to meet a pressing deadline or complete a rush project, or sometimes keep him with me all day for a special activity. Even an hour or two a day when you can be assured of high-quality care for your child while you gain uninterrupted work time can make a huge difference in your attitude and productivity.

If you are unable to locate a suitable professional child-care provider (or don't wish to use one), consider other options that will satisfy you and your child. A high-school-age babysitter can care for your children right in your home during those sometimes-difficult late-afternoon hours or give you a chance to catch up on weekends. Perhaps you have a nearby relative who is happy to spend time with your child on occasion—or even on a regular schedule. Babysitting trade-offs—where you watch a friend's child a certain number of hours a week in return for the same favor—can be quite effective, although my experience has been that it's invariably my turn on a day when I'm struggling to complete a project on deadline. Also, nonworking parents may not be understanding of or sympathetic to your work constraints, and this may cause friction in such an arrangement. Counting on your spouse to care for the children so that you can get work done during evenings or weekends is certainly reasonable, but it does cut into the time the two of you have together. As I mentioned, I've tried nearly every one of these arrangements, with varying degrees of success. It finally dawned on me that I was guilty of the "supermom" syndrome—trying to do a full-time job while providing full-time care to my children. Once I was able to conquer the feeling that I should, somehow, be able to do it all, I realized that being able to count on a certain number of hours of high-quality child care was very beneficial to both my work and my parenting.

Being a home-based worker gives you wonderful opportunities to participate in your children's lives—much more so than you could if you were tied to a rigid schedule or worked for someone other than yourself. I've always enjoyed volunteering in my children's classrooms—the teachers are glad to have assistance, and I've had the chance to observe my kids in a different environment and contribute to their learning. As the owner of my business, I am able to set aside several hours a week for this activity, if I so choose—no explanations or excuses are necessary! My children are free to invite friends over after school or plan an afternoon activity, knowing I'm around. During the summer, they enjoy a relaxed schedule. We plan regular outings together, but they spend a good part of their summers very much like I spent mine as a child—hanging around the neighborhood, playing with friends, running under the sprinkler, riding bikes, playing ball in the street. So many kids today live very structured lives, conforming to their parents' work schedules—I'm glad I can give this freedom to my children.

Your Spouse

This one's a Catch-22. If your spouse is supportive, encouraging, and understanding of the time you devote to your business, it's natural for you to take advantage of his or her willingness to let you put the business first. On the other hand, if your spouse is resentful of the time it takes to run your business and angry at you for not spending time with him or her, your very natural reaction might be to become angry and withhold your time and companionship. A third possibility is that your spouse is totally uninterested in your business and really doesn't enjoy talking about it—which may be difficult for you because it consumes such a big part of your life.

Even before you start your business, have a discussion with your spouse or partner to talk about these issues. Agreeing about time commitments, priorities, and scheduling ahead of time can greatly reduce conflicts. As your business grows, continue communicating with each other, and make adjustments as necessary to keep your relationship on the front burner. For your part, honoring any agreements is important to keeping your spouse supportive. For instance, if you discuss ahead of time that you will work a traditional 9:00 to 5:00 business day and then disappear at 7:00 P.M. to finish a project on deadline, it's understandable that your spouse would be upset. If it's important for both you and your spouse that one of you cares for your children at all times, then don't expect to do much productive work until your spouse gets home. If the arrangement isn't working, sit down to talk about it and make mutual decisions about changes.

My husband, Bob, is totally supportive of the time and effort I put into my business, but he also likes to know that I place a priority on our relationship. As a couple, we've tried several solutions for ensuring "quality time" together—Saturday-night "date nights," the hour after the children's bedtime, weekend outings for just the two of us. Lately we seem to be less structured in our approach, but the common priority of creating some regular time together keeps us on track.

Your Friends

Spending time in social activities can become a low-priority item when competing with demands from business, children, home, and spouse. Good friends will understand that you're busy, but taking regular opportunities to talk and spend time with them will keep your friendships alive and also be a refreshing and relaxing break for you.

Through my networking associations with businesspeople around the country, I've learned that the challenge of combining business with home life is present for all of us, yet unique to our individual circumstances. Networking provides opportunities to share problems and solutions, and just knowing others are in the same boat helps, somehow, to make your own situation more tolerable.

CHAPTER NINE

LIVING YOUR VISION

There is only one success—to be able to spend your life
in your own way.

— CHRISTOPHER MORLEY

ike children, businesses have varying needs at different stages
from infancy through childhood, adolescence, and into adult-
hood. As your company's "parent," it's up to you to keep in mind
its needs and capabilities through these stages and continually
plan for the future.

MANAGING THE GROWTH OF YOUR BUSINESS

Your days of being overwhelmed by work may seem far down the road.
When you first start your business, it's very natural to invest large
amounts of time and energy—almost nothing seems like it's too much
effort. Every job is accepted, every client welcomed. And you'll rejoice
when your ability and hard work begin to pay off with more clients, more
work, and bigger projects.

But it may get to be too much. When you find yourself in a stressful
time-crunch, trying to juggle the competing demands of business, children, partner, friends, and other commitments, just getting through the
day can seem like a monumental accomplishment. If you're lucky, these
hectic spells come in cycles, with more normal periods in between when

you can put life back into balance again. That's the goal in running your own business—achieving the balance that *you* orchestrate and control.

If, on the other hand, you find that the pressure is constant and the scales are always tipped toward the "too busy" side, it's time to think about ways to restore the balance. Do a self-assessment: Is the business running you? Are you trying to be all things to everybody, proving that you can be superwoman or superman? Some of us take an almost perverse pride in living that old army slogan—"We get more done before 9:00 A.M. than most people do in an entire day." It's good to be busy, productive, and in demand, but are you happy? Is your family content? Does your life have balance?

Below are some possible solutions to managing growth, depending on your own unique circumstances:

- Increase your child-care or babysitting coverage to give you more productive work time—but be sure to compensate by being fully present when you *do* spend time with your children.

- Get help! It might be a sensible time for you to consider hiring an employee—either a skilled desktop publisher, to handle some of the production work, or perhaps an administrative assistant, someone who can manage such tasks as billing, making follow-up phone calls and deliveries, filing, running errands, and ordering supplies. Or find a subcontractor who can do the bulk of your text entering, leaving you the more creative design and formatting work.

- Establish a mutual referral network among similar businesses in your area. Find people whose skills you respect and feel comfortable referring work to—especially new clients, jobs you don't particularly enjoy, or even a good client whose deadlines have become too demanding. Referrals can be rewarded by a fixed amount or percentage payment, or you might prefer not to involve any payments but merely refer cooperatively.

- Extend deadlines and refuse rush jobs.

- Upgrade your computer system if it is slowing you down.

- Invest in software training so that you're not wasting time and getting frustrated trying to produce work that is beyond your current abilities.

- Examine all your outside commitments, both work-related and personal. Is it time to quit the church choir? Should you continue to play in two softball leagues? Is that business organization really worth the time you spend in weekly lunch meetings? This is not to suggest that you should exclude everything from your life but work and family, but sometimes—being the efficient overachievers that many of us are—we take on more responsibilities than we can, or really want to, handle.

- Spend about a week tracking your time—the minutes of every hour of every day. This will give you a precise view of how your life is balanced (or unbalanced). You might be working seventy hours a week—or it might be forty but feel like seventy because of constant interruptions. You may be dismayed to discover that you spend less than an hour a day with your children—and even less with your spouse. Perhaps volunteer activities take up ten hours a week—is this where you want the balance to be? If you spend an hour or more a day in personal phone conversations, think about whether this is by conscious choice. In short, before making any changes first establish how it is that you are spending your time right now.

If you do decide to make changes to better manage your growing business and busy life, stay focused on the reasons you started your business in the first place—and keep those goals in the forefront as you make your choices. Remember, *you* are in control—now it's up to you to exercise your authority.

THE FUTURE OF DESKTOP PUBLISHING

Still in its infancy, DTP technology has caused a revolution in the way printed pages are produced. The scope of the changes over the last decade has been truly staggering, and as each change fuels more innovation, the pace continues to accelerate. Though it may be impossible to predict the future, we can make some educated guesses about what lies ahead for our industry:

- The worlds of desktop publishing and printing will come closer and closer together. Already there are printers capable of working directly from computer disks, eliminating the need for paper or film output, color separations, and other prepress functions.

- Advances in both printing technology and desktop color will make color commonplace in everyday business documents.

- Computer hardware and software will continue to grow more powerful, faster, more complex, and fuller-featured.

- Sharing of computer files and information via modem and eventually digital lines may make this medium as commonly used as the telephone.

- Multimedia, video, and other active means of communications will continue to grow as they become easier and less expensive to use.

- Desktop publishers will produce increasingly complex, sophisticated, high-quality documents of every type and variety.

- Skilled communicators—those able to present words and pictures effectively, correctly, and attractively—will continue to be in demand. The "paperless" society envisioned by futurists not long ago shows no signs of developing!

And how does your personal vision, your home-based desktop publishing empire, fit into this constantly developing picture? That's up to you! Remember, you control your own destiny. *You* make the decisions about equipment to buy, market niches to pursue, training to acquire, clients to accept. You may choose to be an innovator, forging ahead with each new technological upgrade, or you may establish a comfortable and profitable niche providing less advanced DTP services.

It's easy to be intimidated by the frighteningly fast changes taking place, but it's important to keep focused on your own personal vision—your reason for starting your business, your hopes and dreams for the future, the life you envision for yourself and your family. This vision will guide you as you make sometimes-difficult decisions about the directions in which to steer your business—directions that may involve technology not yet invented!

Consider conducting an annual review and goal-setting session based on your business activity in the past year. Review your business plan and reflect on whether you are still committed to the stated goals or if they need revision. Give some thought to where you expect changes to occur in the coming year; establish goals and a plan to achieve them. Keep abreast of business and technological changes so that your plan is well informed. And finally, assess whether your business is fulfilling your personal needs: Are you happy? Is your family content? Is your income satisfactory? Is your stress level manageable? Running a home-based desktop publishing business can be an ideal combination of challenge and reward that provides daily satisfaction. In such a rapidly changing field, new opportunities are constantly presenting themselves. Be on the alert and ready to take advantage of them and you will have a successful business that continues to meet your unique needs and fulfill your personal goals—whatever they may be.

APPENDIX

> Knowledge is power. — **FRANCIS BACON**

BOOKS

Getting Business to Come to You, Paul and Sarah Edwards and Laura Clampitt Douglas (Jeremy P. Tarcher/Perigee, 1991)

Guerrilla Marketing and *Guerrilla Marketing Attack,* Jay Conrad Levinson (Houghton Mifflin Company, 1984, 1989)

How to Open and Operate a Home-based Secretarial Services Business, Jan Melnik (Globe Pequot Press, 1994)

Looking Good in Print: A Guide to Basic Design for Desktop Publishing, Roger C. Parker (Ventana Press, Inc., 1988[a])

Pricing Guide for Desktop Publishing Services, 4th ed., Robert Brenner (Brenner Information Group, 1995[a, b])

Understanding Desktop Color, Michael Kieran (Desktop Publishing Associates, 1994[a])

[a] available at a discount to members of the National Association of Desktop Publishers

[b] available at a discount to members of the National Association of Secretarial Services

CREDIT CARD

Discover/Novus Services, 800–347–2000. My experience with this company is that it is an excellent source for obtaining merchant status without difficult and time-consuming bank approvals. They have no prejudice against home-based businesses. In order to accept MasterCard and Visa as well as Discover/Novus, it is necessary to purchase or lease an electronic credit card terminal.

GUIDES AND CATALOGS

Creating a Client Newsletter: Content·Design·Production·Distribution. Louise Kursmark, 1995. 9847 Catalpa Woods Court, Cincinnati, OH 45242. (eight-page booklet plus sample newsletters)

DTP Direct, desktop publishing catalog—graphics, imaging and prepress solutions. 5198 West 76th Street, Edina, MN 55439, 800–890–9374.

Font & Function, Adobe Corp.'s type catalog—an excellent resource. PO Box 6458, Salinas, CA 93912-6458; 800–445–8787.

MacConnection/PC Connection, 800–800–1111. An outstanding mail order source for all things computer-related (and computers, too). Great customer service and technical support, twenty-four hours a day.

PrePress Direct, catalog for desktop publishing and prepress professionals. 11 Mt. Pleasant Avenue, East Hanover, NJ 07936-9925, 800–443–6600.

Resources! Kathy Keshemberg, 1995. Dept. LK, 302 East Murray Avenue, Appleton, WI 54915. (packet of sample marketing materials, invoices, and business forms)

ORGANIZATIONS

National Association of Desktop Publishers, 462 Old Boston Street, Topsfield, MA 01983-1232, 800–874–4113. Yearly membership: $95. Includes subscription to the *Journal*, described below, as well as a bimonthly members-only newsletter, *Inside Report,* and additional services such as the BuyDirect Program, offering hardware and software discounts; the Bookstore, providing discounts on an excellent selection of DTP-related books; and the Member HelpLine Network, which provides free technical support by phone and a quarterly directory of volunteer specialists.

National Association of Secretarial Services, 3637 Fourth Street North, St. Petersburg, FL 33704, 800-237-1462. Includes monthly newsletter, annual conference, and a nationwide network of members willing to share information and provide assistance.

PERIODICALS

Adobe Magazine, 411 First Avenue S., Seattle, WA 98104-2871, fax (206) 343-3273. Bimonthly, free to registered owners of Adobe products or $35/year. An excellent resource, providing information for readers at all levels of expertise.

Bootstrappin' Entrepreneur, Suite B261, 8726 South Sepulveda Boulevard, Los Angeles, CA 90045-4082, (310) 568-9861. Subscriptions $30/year. A quarterly "newsletter for individuals with great ideas and a little bit of cash." Its twelve-page format is tightly packed with worthwhile information, with no specific industry focus.

Byte magazine, 1 Phoenix Mill Lane, Peterborough, NH. Monthly, $30/year.

Home Office Computing, 411 Lafayette Street, New York, NY 10003, 800-288-7812. Newsstand price $2.95, subscriptions discounted substantially depending on length of subscription (e.g., twelve issues for $19.97, twenty-four issues for $31.97). HOC is a tremendously useful, interesting, and well-written magazine that offers advice and information on all aspects of small and home-based businesses.

MacUser, Ziff-Davis Publishing Company, One Park Avenue, New York, NY 10016. Monthly, $27/year.

MacWorld, PO Box 54529, Boulder, CO 80322-4529, 800–288–6848. Monthly, $30/year.

NADTP Journal (a publication of the National Association of Desktop Publishers, see *"Organizations"*), 462 Old Boston Street, Topsfield, MA 01983-1232, 800–874–4113. Subscriptions (without full NADTP membership) $48/year for twelve issues. The *Journal* is a very good source for high-end desktop publishing information and assumes the reader has substantial knowledge in the field.

The Page, 9420 Bunsen Parkway, Suite 300, Louisville, KY 40220, 800–223–8720. Subscriptions $69/year. A twenty-page monthly newsletter offering illustrated tips and design information specifically related to desktop publishing.

PC Magazine, Ziff-Davis Publishing Company, One Park Avenue, New York, NY 10016-5802. Biweekly, $50/year.

Technique magazine, PO Box 9164, Hyattsville, MD 20781-9164, 800–272–7377. Monthly, $39/year. Good source for basic DTP and design information (probably too basic for more advanced DTP users).

The Word Advantage, Dept. LK, PO Box 718, Durham, CT 06422, (860) 349–1343. Subscriptions $30/year. A quarterly newsletter offering "creative ideas and marketing strategies for those who work with words." Though not focused directly on desktop publishing, this newsletter is an outstanding source, particularly for marketing ideas that can be used by nearly any business. And if you deal extensively in "words" (writing, editing, typesetting), you will find a great deal in every issue. (I am a Contributing Editor to this publication.)

SPECIALTY PAPERS

The following companies offer specialty and/or preprinted papers in a variety of formats, including brochures, business cards, postcards, note cards, labels, letterhead, and envelopes. Many offer other laser-printer and desktop publishing products as well, such as transparencies, plain laser labels, binding and laminating systems, product layout software, and certificate frames. I recommend keeping these catalogs on file and browsing through them when you need to use these products for a project. In addition, for a small charge most of the companies offer a "sampler kit" of most or all of their papers—a good design inspiration.

Beaver Prints, 305 Main Street, Bellwood, PA 16617, 800-923-2837.

Icon Graphix, 6460 N. Lincoln Avenue, Lincolnwood, IL 60645, 800-426-6151.

Idea Art, PO Box 291505, Nashville, TN 32779-1505, 800-433-2278. (All papers are recycled.)

LeDesktop, PO Box 45000, Phoenix, AZ 85064, 800-LE DESKTOP (No preprinted designs but an outstanding selection of unusual and high-quality papers.)

On Paper, PO Box 1365, Elk Grove Village, IL 60009-1365, 800-820-2299.

Paper Access, 23 West 18 Street, New York, NY 10011, 800-727-3701. (Good selection of specialty papers; fewer preprinted designs.)

Paper Adventures, PO Box 04393, Milwaukee, WI 53204-0393, 800-727-0699.

Paper Direct, PO Box 1514, Secaucus, NJ 07096-1514, 800-272-7377. (The industry leader in preprinted papers, with the most formats and among the best designs.)

Premier Papers, PO Box 64785, St. Paul, MN 55164, 800-843-0414.

Queblo, 1000 Florida Avenue, Hagerstown, MD 21741, 800-523-9080.

Quill Laser & Inkjet Paper & Supplies, PO Box 94080, Palatine, IL 60094-4080, 800-789-1331. (Also an outstanding source for office supplies of all kinds; ask for their complete catalog.)

INDEX

A

accountant
services of, 41, 64
accounting
at start-up, 60
systems, 146–48, 149–51
advertising
business journal, 97–98
newspaper, 97–98
ongoing, 94–98
radio and television, 98
start-up, 62
Yellow Pages, 94–96
appointments
billing for, 157–58
scheduling, 156–57
attorney
services of, 41, 64
attracting clients, 93–111
automobile expense, 65

B

back-up system, 52
procedures, 148–49
software, 52
billable hours annually, 69
billing and invoicing, 146–48
books and periodicals, 20–21, 35–36
business, home-based
advantages, 5
distractions and interruptions, 15
integrating home and business, 201–10
isolation, 14
managing, 201–10

pitfalls, 5
safety issues, 85
specific skills needed, 13–15
with children, 205–9
business cards
as marketing tools, 123
designing, 58
start-up, 58
business growth, managing, 211–13
business journal advertising, 97
business name, 36–38
business plan
outline, 73–75
parts, 73–75
using, 75–76
why you need one, 72–73
business registration, 38
business sign, 61
business structure, 39–41
corporation, 40
limited-liability company, 40
partnership, 40
sole proprietorship, 40
business use of home, 64

C

calendar, 133
capital acquisitions, 63
cash flow, managing, 151–54
CD-ROM, 52–53
checking account, 61
child care options, 208–9
children
strategies for home-based business,
205–9

Client File, 136
Client Information File, 134–35
Client Information/Agreement, 136, 137
Client Sign-off Sheet, 138
client
    appointments, 156–57
    database, 134–35
    disks, accepting, 176–77
    files, 148–49
    meeting space, 86
    newsletter, 118–21
    objections, 163
    presentations, 162–64
    problems, 112–13
    relationships, 156–57
    satisfaction survey, 114, 117
client information
    gathering and maintaining, 133–39
client work, ownership of, 178
clients
    appreciation program, 113–15
    attracting, 93–98
    definition of, 91
    increased sales to, 114–20
    meetings at their office, 158
    problems with, 203–5
    referrals from, 101–2
    surveying, 114, 117
    thanking, 102, 113–14
clip art, 54
cold calling, 103–5
collecting money due, 152–53
competition
    analyzing, 41–42
computer
    problems and resources, 154–56
    retailer, 22
computer equipment, 45, 48–49
    keyboard, 49
    monitor, 49
    scanner, 51
conferences, 21
credit, extending, 153–54
customer service, 15
    retaining clients through, 111–13

D

database, client, 134
deadlines, meeting, 132–33
desktop publishers, background of, 4, 19
desktop publishing (DTP)
    definition, 2
    design guidelines, 170–75
    future of, 213–14
    history, 2–3
    home-based, 5
    practitioners, 3
    products, 4
    skills required, 7–10
    software, 49
    standards for, 180–97
    work process, 197–200
direct mail marketing, 105–7
disks
    accepting, 176
    Guidelines for preparing disk files, 177
    providing, 176–79
drop boxes, 84–85

E

earnings, expected, 66
ergonomic issues, 88–89
Estimating Worksheet, 181
estimating costs, 164, 165–66
    for specific DTP projects, 180–97
    sample Estimating Worksheet, 181
exercise, 89
Expense Summary charts, 67–68

F

fax
    dedicated line, 55
    features, 56–57
fees
    different hourly rates, 70
    establishing, 66, 69–71
    hourly, 71
    minimum, 69–70
    pricing rationale, 70–71
    project, 71
    raising annually, 70

file compression, 52
financial record-keeping, 149–51
financing
   bank, 75–76
    credit cards, 76
   home equity loan, 76
   relatives and friends, 76
   savings, 76
   using business plan, 75–76
follow up
   to direct mail marketing, 106–7
   to outstanding accounts, 152–53
fonts, 54
furniture, 54–55

G

graphics software, 49
growth of business, 211–13

H

hard disk, capacity, 49
health insurance, 65
health, 15
   maintenance of, 88–89
home-based business
   advantages, 5
   distractions and interruptions, 13
   integrating home and business, 201–10
   isolation, 14
   managing, 201–10
   pitfalls, 5–6
   specific skills needed, 13–15
   with children, 205–9
home office, setting up, 81–89
hourly rates, 69–70

I

IBM-compatible computers, 48
insurance
   business, 61
   disability, 61
   health, 65
   liability, 61
invoicing
   billing terms, 146, 153

extending credit, 154
follow-up, 152–53
procedures, 146–48
sample invoice, 147
timeliness, 152

J

Job Element Checklists, 180–97

L

lead time, 132
leads group, 20
legal and regulatory issues, 38–39

M

Macintosh computers, 48
maintenance agreements, 65–66
   computer, 155
marketing
   and selling DTP services, 91–125
   cold calling, 103–5
   developing materials, 121–24
   direct mail, 105–7
   networking, 99–101
   publicity, 107–111
   start-up, 62
   strategy, 91–93
   telephone, 158–61
   through client newsletter, 118–21
   through client presentations, 162–64
   to existing clients, 115–21
   with a portfolio, 121–26
   word of mouth, 98–99
mission statement, 17–18

N

naming business, 36–38
networking
   group assistance, 20
   informal, 21
   marketing through, 99–101
newsletter
   marketing through, 118–21
   sample newsletter, 119–20
newspaper advertising, 97–98

43
45
44

s, 44
technical expertise, 43
typography and layout, 43

O

office
    decoration, 88
    essentials, 86–88
    safety, 85–86
    set-up, 81–89
    space, 81–82
office equipment, 54–60
office supplies
    sources, 57
    start-up costs, 59
    start-up, 58
online services
    information from, 22
organizations
organizing
    client information, 133–38
    office, 86–88
    work, 128–33
ownership of client work, 178

P

paper
    office supplies, 57–58
    preprinted designer papers, 122–23
periodicals, 20–21
part-time business, 76–77
personal safety, 85–86
photocopier, 57
planning checklists, 78–80
policies, 136–38
    sample Policy Statement, 139
portfolio
    developing and using, 124–26

presentations
    to clients, 162–64
    to community organizations,
press release, 107–10
pricing
    rationale, 70–71
    for DTP projects, 180–97
printer
    working with, 103–4
productivity, 13
professional identity
    developing materials, 121–24
    your business's, 58
professional image, 14
professional organizations
    networking through, 100–101
Project Schedule, 128–32
    sample, 129
Project Tracker, 142–45
proposals and estimates
    preparing, 165–66
    sample letter, 167–68
publicity, 107–111
    angles and hooks, 108, 110
    communicating with writers and
        editors, 110
    pitching a story, 109–10
    sample press release, 109
    television and radio, 110

Q

quality
    retaining clients through, 111–13

R

RAM, 2, 49
rate structure
    establishing, 62–66
    Pricing Guide, 62
    rationale, 71
record-keeping
    financial, 149–51
    start-up system, 60

referrals
  cultivating, 101–2
  to subcontractors, 32
  word of mouth, 98–99
retaining clients, 111–15
retirement planning, 65

S

safety, personal, 85–86
salary
  expectations, 63
  projecting, 63
selling
  and marketing DTP services, 91–126
  cold calling, 103–5
  developing sales materials, 121–24
  direct mail, 105–7
  networking, 99–101
  publicity, 107–111
  telephone, 158–61
  through client presentations, 162–64
  to existing clients, 115–21
  with a portfolio, 124–26
  word of mouth, 98–99
seminars, 21
separating business and home lives,
  203–4
service
  as competitive advantage, 71
service bureaus
  computer compatibility, 48
service mix
  charts, 46–47
  fast service, 43
  graphic design, 43
  including subcontracted services, 45
  large projects, 44
  low rates, 43
  selecting, 42–45
  small business, 44
  technical expertise, 43
  typography and layout, 43
  75-percent rule, 69–70, 130
signage, 61

skills
  building upon, 17–18
  business management, 10–13
  computer, 8, 12
  developing and improving, 19–22
  editorial, 10
  graphic design, 8–9
  marketing, 11–12
  page layout, 7–8
  personal characteristics, 15–16
  printing knowledge, 9
  technical, 7–10
  typesetting, 9
  typing/word processing, 10
  typography, 9
Small Business Administration (SBA), 20
software
  clip art, 54
  desktop publishing, 49–50
  file back-up, 52
  file compression, 52
  fonts, 54
  graphics, 49
  OCR, 51
  start-up, 49–50
  virus protection, 52
specializing, 18
standards for DTP projects, 180–97
  brochure, 182–84
  flyer, 195–96
  letterhead, envelope, business card,
    190–91
  menu, 192–94
  newsletter, 187–88
start-up costs
  estimating, 63–65
  Expense Summary charts, 67–68
start-up needs
  computer equipment, 45, 48–49
  cost estimates, 53
  keyboard, 49
  monitor, 49
  printers, 51
  scanner, 51–52
  software, 49–50

using, 174
Subchapter-S corporation, 40
subcontractors and vendors
    advantages 23, 32
    disadvantages, 23–24
    expectations, 28
    experiences, 33
    locating and utilizing, 23–33
    sample scripts, 25–26
    Subcontractor Job Summary 29–31

T

taxes
    income (federal and state), 63–64
    personal property, 39
    sales, 39
    self-employment, 63
telephone, 55–56
    answering, 56, 204–5
    cordless, 55
    fax, 56–57
    hold button, 55
    sales, 158–61
time
    for children, 205–8
    for yourself, 202
    management, 15
    tracking, 142–45
tracking
    expense, 151
    financial, 149–51
    profit centers, 149–50
    time, 142–45

training, 20–22
    Training Resources grid, 19
typography guidelines, 171–74

V

value, 71
vendors and subcontractors
    advantages 23, 32
    disadvantages, 23–24
    expectations, 28
    experiences, 33
    locating and utilizing, 23–33
    sample scripts, 25–26
    Subcontractor Job Summary 28–31
virus protection, 52

W

Windows, 48
word of mouth marketing, 98–99
work systems
    developing a process, 197–200
    keeping order, 141–47
    organizational, 141–42
work time
    structuring, 140–41
    tracking, 142–45
WYSIWYG, 2

Y

Yellow Pages advertising
    analyzing competitors, 41
    advertising, 94–96
    categories, 95
    discounts, 96, 97

Z

zoning, 38–39